JESUS THE GREAT PHYSICIAN

JESUS THE GREAT PHYSICIAN

Dr W F Hannay

RITCHIE

John Ritchie Publishing

40 Beansburn, Kilmarnock, Scotland

ISBN-13: 978 1 912522 48 4

Copyright © 2019 by John Ritchie Ltd.
40 Beansburn, Kilmarnock, Scotland

www.ritchiechristianmedia.co.uk

Typeset by John Ritchie Ltd., Kilmarnock
Printed by Bell & Bain Ltd., Glasgow

To my wife Gillian

ENDORSEMENTS

Having commenced reading the book, I have almost finished it in one sitting. It is an interesting and insightful book that gives us a thought-provoking look at the healing miracles of the Saviour and a deeper appreciation of the Lord Jesus in His person and work.

Drew Allen
GP, Annalong, County Down, Northern Ireland

This is a thoughtful and thorough summary offering careful analysis of each of the healing miracles of the Lord Jesus as presented in the New Testament. Walter Hannay has combined a careful study of the scripture record with his wide medical experience and the result is a superb account of this aspect of the ministry of Christ. His insight into some of the unusual clinical presentations brings a new perspective to this fascinating topic. Not only is this concise volume easy to read it is an excellent reference for further study. Recommended!

David J. Galloway MB ChB MD DSc FRCS[Glasg] FRCS[Ed] FACS FRCP[Edin] FACP FRCPI FAMM FAIS FCSSL FICP FIMSA

Honorary Professor, College of Medical Veterinary and Life Sciences, University of Glasgow and Immediate Past President, Royal College of Physicians and Surgeons of Glasgow.

Dr Hannay draws on his 40 years experience as a medical practitioner to provide many helpful and unusual insights into the medical miracles of the Lord Jesus to give us a fresh vivid understanding of our Saviour's healing ministry. Highly recommended!

Dr David MacAdam
Chitokoloki Mission Station Hospital, Zambia

Christians have always been intrigued and fascinated by the healing miracles of Jesus. Unlike other therapies and other so-called miracle cures, they were clear signs, instantaneous, complete, unassociated with other remedies, and non-recurrent.

Looking at the Gospels through a twenty-first century lens, it is always difficult to know the diagnoses involved and the mechanisms of healing. Just like Jesus' contemporaries we can only stand amazed.

Doctor Hannay has carried out a thorough study, which includes perspectives and writings from physicians of the ancient world. I am delighted to say that the book is both scholarly and yet readily understandable to the non-medical reader.

I regard this book as a must-read for the Christian health worker who wants to understand Jesus' healing miracles from a Gospel viewpoint. It will advance both our knowledge of Jesus and desire for a compassionate heart to a sick humanity.

Jonathan Redden MA MB BS FRCS

Retired consultant orthopaedic surgeon, Doncaster

ABBREVIATIONS

KJV	Authorised Version (King James Version).
NIV	New International Version.
NKJV	New King James Version.

ACKNOWLEDGEMENTS

Mr Fraser Munro for his encouragement, advice and overseeing of the text.

My son Philip and his wife Laura for help with computing problems.

Mrs Ella MacDonald and Mrs Rae Lind for suggestions regarding the text.

Contents

Preface

Everyone needs a Doctor at some time, even if it is just to sign a death certificate! This book is written with a view of Jesus Christ as not only a Physician but the greatest Physician who ever lived.

Thirty-seven miracles are recorded in the Gospels and as Mary Fairchild says: *"None were performed randomly, for amusement or for show. Each was accompanied by a message and either met a serious human need or confirmed Christ`s identity and authority as the Son of God"*.[1]

Having been a Doctor for over forty years, I have viewed the healing miracles of the Lord Jesus in the Gospels under medical categories as seen from a modern classification of disease. Not every miracle is therefore included - only those I see in a category of disease or medical specialty. I have added some thoughts at times relevant to the miracle.

The review is limited to the four Gospels although in the first chapter of the Acts of the Apostles, the Physician Luke tells us that in his Gospel he recorded the things that Jesus *"began both to do and teach, until the day in which He was taken up"* (verses 1-2) to Heaven. He thus infers that Jesus is still doing and teaching through His Apostles in the book of Acts. Two of these are mentioned briefly in the book.

The chapters have been arranged in chronological order rather in order of any perceived importance.

---

[1]Mary Fairchild, see https://www.thoughtco.com/miracles-of-jesus-700158, accessed March 2018

Introduction:
The Great Physician

Jesus of Nazareth considered Himself as a Physician. This is clear from His self-references in Scripture. For example: *"Ye will surely say unto Me this proverb, Physician heal Thyself..."*[2] and again: *"They that are whole need not a physician; but they that are sick"*[3] (referring to Himself) and: *"Behold, I cast out demons and perform cures today and tomorrow, and the third day I shall be perfected"*.[4]

The nation of Israel unto which Jesus came should, above all nations, have enjoyed good health. God promised that if they obeyed His Laws they would have none of the diseases they saw in Egypt during the years of their captivity there.[5] But, if they did not observe His Laws or fear Him then He would bring severe diseases upon them. These diseases would be like those they had seen in Egypt or even worse in intensity, duration and variety.[6] They did not obey His Laws as a Nation and disease was rampant in Israel when the Son of God came.

The priest in Old Testament times would be the Physician, diagnosing disease, enforcing Public Health Laws of hygiene and quarantine and judging occasion and fitness for rehabilitation. Andrew Bonar remarks in his commentary on Leviticus: *"In the cases where disease is prescribed for by special rules, Aaron is joined with Moses. This is because a priest - a High Priest - ought to have more compassion while hearing the tone of pity in which the Lord spoke of man`s misery."* [7] The empathy of the priest Physician is recorded.

Of course, in the Old Testament God is referred to as *'Jehovah–Rophecha'*.[8] In the text, it says: *"I am the Lord that healeth thee"*. Henry Dyer in his book *'Jehovah's Name'*, quotes an old translation: *"I am Jehovah thy Physician"*.[9] Also, in Psalm 103 verse 3, God is said to heal all our diseases. As the famous Physician Sir William Osler once said: *"I treated the patient, God healed him."*[10]

In the prophesy of Isaiah,[11] the Kingdom of God is described as manifesting the glory of the Lord in the opening of the eyes of the blind and the ears of the deaf, the dramatic curing of the lame and the dumb speaking. This was seen in the ministry of the Lord Jesus as recorded in the Gospels. Hence He is bringing in the Kingdom of God in healing power in His ministry and fulfilling Isaiah's vision, although a fuller manifestation will be seen in the coming Kingdom age.

Matthew in his Gospel tells us in Chapter 4 verse 23 that Jesus was a Teacher, a Preacher and a Physician: *"And Jesus went about all Galilee, teaching in their synagogues, and preaching the gospel of the kingdom, and healing all manner of sickness and all manner of disease among the people"*. Matthew prioritises teaching and preaching but also expands upon the Lord's ministry of healing.

Matthew seems to divide the healing miracles of Jesus into external and internal causes by repeatedly differentiating the words *"sickness"* and *"diseases"* as in the above verse but also in Chapter 9: *"Then Jesus went about all the cities and villages, teaching in their synagogues, preaching the gospel of the kingdom, and healing every sickness and every disease among the people."*[12] Also in Chapter 10: *"And when He had called His twelve disciples to Him, He gave them power over unclean spirits, to cast them out, and to heal all kinds of sickness and all kinds of disease."*[13]

W.E Vine says the Greek word *'malakia'* means: *"primarily softness, hence debility, and is found in Matthew only in the New Testament"*.[14] It is translated as *'bodily weakness'* in the *Englishman's Greek New*

Testament.[15] *'Nosos'*, akin to the Latin *'Nocere'* means, according to Vine: *"to injure and is the regular word for disease"*.

Thus it seems that Matthew the careful 'Civil Servant' distinguishes the two words in recording the healing miracles of the Lord Jesus. He would hardly use repetition of the two words for the same types of disease.

Matthew the tax collector, in keeping with his former professional style, seems to love lists! This is seen in other Scriptures in his Gospel. For example:

- the genealogy of the Lord in Chapter 1
- the Beatitudes in Chapter 5 verses 3-12 and
- the Parables of the Kingdom in Chapter 13.

Thus, in Chapter 4 verse 24 he records in summary group-list samples of healings Jesus did – *"sick people who were afflicted with various diseases and torments, and those who were demon-possessed, epileptics, and paralytics"* – and records that He healed them all. He did not just treat them - He healed them. No case was too difficult or advanced.

The Lord Jesus Himself, of course, never contracted disease in the process. He could handle the leper without contracting leprosy and the fevered without contagion. Psalm 91 verse 10 had prophesied: *"No evil shall befall you, nor shall any plague come near your dwelling"*. His body was prepared by God for entry into a world of sickness: *"A body hast Thou prepared Me"* (Hebrews 10:5). He was the Holy One of God and *"separate from sinners"*.[16]

As a functioning Priest/Physician after the pattern of Aaron, although genealogically of the tribe of Judah, Jesus had none of the physical features recorded in Leviticus 21 verse 21 which would disqualify Him from service.

It is noteworthy that Jesus had the approach and attitude of the perfect Physician. He does not invade personal privacy but asks permission from the individual to help. An example would be the case of the blind man in Jericho when Jesus says: *"What do you want Me to do for you?"*[17] and the man at the pool of Bethesda: *"Do you want to be made well?"*[18] On other occasions, people are brought to Him for help, such as the paralysed man in Mark 2 verse 3, or individuals offering themselves for healing, as the leper in Luke 5.[19] On such occasions, permission has tacitly been granted to the Lord for examination and treatment.

It is said that a Physician is as good as his last consultation! Every consultation with Jesus was good. Every patient went away healed. He had no complaints! That is in itself miraculous! Every patient was a "private" patient but He sent no bills!

He never takes a superior attitude to people - remarkable, as He is above all. He was born into a poor home in a despised town in a remote part of the Roman Empire, lived in a sizable family, was apprenticed as a carpenter before embarking on His public ministry of healing without formal University training. He was, as the Christmas carol *"Once in Royal David`s City"* records, with the *"poor and lowly"* although the Son of God. He could say: *"I am meek and lowly in heart."*[20] He would understand the problems and joys of ordinary people at their level. What suitable qualifications to meet all people in their need, including us!

This Physician was always available for people. He was never off-duty, even when He wished some repose and time for reflection as after the death of John Baptist[21] and the report on the mission of the twelve as reported in Mark 6 verse 31. The multitudes discerned where He was going and were already present before He and the disciples arrived. Instead of ignoring them or dismissing them as the disciples advised later, He had compassion on them and gave them considerable teaching as recorded in Mark 6 verse 34. Luke adds, himself a Physician: *"He received them, and ... healed them that had need of healing"*,[22] healing the sick when on holiday and off-duty!

In Chapter 8 verse 17, Matthew sees Jesus fulfilling the prophesy of Isaiah 53 verse 4 (*"That it might be fulfilled which was spoken by Esaias the prophet, saying, Himself took our infirmities, and bare our sicknesses"*) in His ministry with the implication that He Himself was personal Physician to the Nation of Israel. A rather large practice! Far from being detached from people in His healing ministry, the Lord Jesus had not only personal sympathy but empathy with His patients. The Psalmist says three times: *"The Lord is gracious and full of compassion"*.[23] Jesus is noted for His compassion on the needy:

- see Mark 1 verse 41 - the leper
- and Luke 7 verse 13 - the widow of Nain.

Love was the motive in His work.

- Matthew 14 verse 14 says: He *"was moved with compassion for them, and healed their sick"*.

His healing ministry is linked to His future vicarious suffering for sin, the root cause of disease and suffering and the removal of the curse from the earth. We find the fulfilment of Isaiah 53 verse 4: *"Surely He has borne our griefs and carried our sorrows"*. These works are a demonstration that the kingdom of Satan is being undermined now by His power. As stated already, the physical fruit of the cross will be manifest in the Millennium when there will be scant disease and illness. If such occur, there will be healing with the leaves of the Tree of Life which is for the healing of the Nations or, as some think,[24] the leaves of the Tree will be a preventative therapy in that day. Death at 100 years will be accounted as an untimely death[25] as man will have the potential to live to years approaching 1,000.

In the "New World Order" announced in Revelation 21 verse 4, there will be the total absence of sickness, pain, bereavement and death itself. Adam was forbidden access to the tree of life in Eden lest he live in sin forever. Now access is available to the redeemed. A world with total health! We are so glad that *"These words are faithful and true"*.

Although we see the fulfilment of prophecy and the portents of the age to come in a variety of individual encounters of the Lord Jesus which involve healing, yet in spite of all His works the nation of Israel did not hear or see with their heart and, as Isaiah prophesied in Chapter 6 verse 10, they were not converted and healed. However, the situation will be reversed in a day to come when that nation will say: *"Surely He has borne our griefs and carried our sorrows; ... but He was wounded for our transgressions, He was bruised for our iniquities ... with His stripes we are healed"* (Isaiah 53:4,5). This also applies to all of us today, for verse 6 says: *"All we like sheep have gone astray .... and the Lord has laid on Him the iniquity of us all"*.

Jesus Himself said that He had not come to judge people but to save them. Just as He refused to be involved in legal disputes, so also as a Physician He did not deal with people judgmentally or get involved directly in social or moral causes of disease (Luke 13:1-5 and John 9:1). However, the Lord did warn of the consequences of returning to certain former behaviour, such as in the case of the woman taken in adultery in John 8, the casting out of a demon from a person in Luke 11 verse 26 and the man made to walk after 38 years an invalid in John 5.

To quote Exodus 15 verse 26 again, God says: *"If thou wilt diligently hearken to the voice of the Lord thy God, and wilt do that which is right in His sight, and wilt give ear to His commandments, and keep all His statutes, I will put none of these diseases upon thee, which I have brought upon the Egyptians: for I am the Lord that healeth thee"*. As disease did come upon the Nation of Israel in spite of the health warning, it may come to us too as a result of failure to obey this injunction. How good to know that the *"Year of Jubilee"* according to Leviticus 25 had come with Jesus, as proclaimed by Himself in Luke 4 verses 18-21 with the promise of deliverance, healing, recovery and liberty. We are also reminded in John 1 verse 17 that grace and truth came with Jesus Christ.

The question could be asked: "Did this Great Physician have Medical students?" Mark 3 v 14 tells us that He chose His students *"That they should be with Him, and that He might send them forth to preach, and to have power to heal sicknesses, and to cast out demons"*. In Luke 9 verse 1: *"Then He called His twelve disciples together, and gave them power and authority over all demons, and to cure diseases, and He sent them to preach the kingdom of God, and to heal the sick"*. They are to put into practice what they learned. Again in Luke 10 verse 9 after seventy others are appointed, He says: *"Heal the sick who are there* [in the town] *and tell them, 'The kingdom of God is near to you'"*. We see them further in action after the resurrection of the Lord as recorded in Acts 5 verse 12: *"The Apostles performed many miraculous signs and wonders among the people"*.

Specific examples of healing performed by Peter are found in Acts 9 verses 33 and 34[26] and in Acts 9 verse 40.[27] In the former, Peter comes to the town of Lydda where a man called Aeneas has been paralysed and in bed eight years. He says to him, *"Aenaes, Jesus Christ heals you. Arise and make your bed"*. This is very similar to the way the Master dealt with the paralysed man in Mark 2.[28] In the latter, Peter arrives at Joppa and finds that a lady of the local church called Dorcas has died. When he arrived, he put all the people out of the room where she was lying and after praying says to the dead woman: *"Tabitha, arise"*. When she had opened her eyes she saw Peter and sat up. How very like the raising of the girl in Mark 5 when Jesus put all out save the father and mother and Peter, James and John and said: *"Little girl, I say unto you arise"*. She got up and walked about. The student had absorbed his Master`s teaching.

Someone has said that a Lawyer sees people at their worst, a Minister at their best but a Doctor as they are. The Lord Jesus saw people as they were and He met people at their point of their need, no matter the race, religion or cause of the disease and uniquely made them all perfectly whole.

[2]Luke 4:23

[3]Luke 5:31

[4]Luke 13:32, NKJV

[5]Exodus 15:26

[6]Deuteronomy 28:59-62

[7]Bonar, Andrew, 'A Commentary on the Book of Leviticus' (The Sovereign Grace Book Club, Jay Green, 1959), page 288.

[8]Exodus 15:26

[9]Dyer, Henry, 'Jehovah`s Name' (John Ritchie, Kilmarnock), page 13.

[10]Osler, Sir William - Canadian Physician - 1849-1919

[11]Isaiah 35:5-6

[12]Matthew 9:35, NKJV

[13]Matthew 10:1, NKJV

[14]Vine, W. E., 'Expository Dictionary of Old and New Testament words' (1997, Thomas Nelson Inc. page 309.

[15]The Englishman`s Greek New Testament, Samuel Bagster and Sons Ltd. Third edition

[16]Hebrews 7:26

[17]Luke 17:41, NKJV

[18]John 5:6, NKJV

[19]See Luke 5:12

[20]Matthew 11:29

[21]See Mark 6:29-34

[22]Luke 9:11

[23]See Psalm 111:4, 112:4 and 145:8

[24]Flanigan, Jim, 'Notes on Revelation', Gospel Tract Publications, Glasgow, 1987 page 116

[25]Isaiah 65:20, 22

[26]https://www.biblegateway.com/passage/?search=Acts+9%3A+33&version=KJV

[27]https://www.biblegateway.com/passage/?search=Acts+10%3A+40&version=KJV

[28]https://www.biblegateway.com/passage/?search=mark+2&version=KJV

The 'Impossible' Case
(The virgin birth)

"And it came to pass in those days that a decree went out from Caesar Augustus that all the world should be registered. This census first took place while Quirinius was governing Syria. So all went to be registered, everyone to his own city. Joseph also went up from Galilee, out of the city of Nazareth, into Judea, to the city of David, which is called Bethlehem, because he was of the house and lineage of David, to be registered with Mary, his betrothed wife, who was with child. So it was, that while they were there, the days were completed for her to be delivered. And she brought forth her firstborn Son, and wrapped Him in swaddling cloths, and laid Him in a manger, because there was no room for them in the inn."

Luke 2 verses 1-7

The birth of Jesus Christ was unique in human history. It has been said that there have been four modes of entrance into the world:

- the creation of man
- the formation of woman
- the procreation of society
- the incarnation of the Son of God.

God kept His masterpiece till the end. (One wonders if Satan will produce *his* masterpiece in the Antichrist.)

That a virgin would conceive and have a son was prophesied as early as Genesis 3 verse 15 when it was said that the "Seed of the woman" would come to bruise the serpent's head. Isaiah the prophet confirmed this statement in chapter 7 verse 14 when he said: *"Behold, the virgin shall conceive, and bear a son, and shall call His name Immanuel"*. This prophecy applied first of all to King Ahaz as a special sign (v11) but the fulfilment was in the birth of Jesus Christ at Bethlehem in Judaea by the virgin called Mary.[29]

After Mary received the news of her Divine choice to be the mother of the Son of God, she asked the all-searching question: *"How shall this be, seeing I know not a man?"* (Luke 1:34). She received the answer:

- *"The Holy Spirit will come upon you"* - that was for conception
- *"the power of the Highest will overshadow you"* - that was for protection of mother and child -
- and *"that Holy thing that shall be born of you will be called the Son of God"*. That refers to the Lord's incarnation (Luke 1:35).

"Great is the mystery of godliness: God was manifest in flesh" writes Paul to Timothy later in 1 Timothy 3 verse 16. *"The Word became flesh and tabernacled among us"* writes John in chapter 1 verse 14 of his Gospel.

It is said that the number of words used by Luke when referring to pregnancy and barrenness are almost as large as those used by Hippocrates. It is, therefore, interesting to note the various words used in the text. In Luke 1 verse 31, the Greek word used is *"gastri"* when the Archangel Gabriel addresses Mary regarding her conception. The same word is used in the Septuagint in Isaiah 7 verse 14. The word *"koilia"* is otherwise used in these early chapters of Luke. He himself uses it in verse 41 and Elisabeth uses it in verse 42 and verse 44; this being a more specific term.[30] The word *"gastri"* is used by Luke later in chapter 21 verse 23 translated in the AV: *"with child"* or: "those who are pregnant".[31]

How accurate was the fulfilment of the prophecies concerning the birth of the Messiah! The place where it was to occur, not just the manner, was also prophesied. Bethlehem in Judah, predicted the prophet Micah 735 years before in chapter 5 v 2 of his prophecy. How was it to be accomplished since the parents lived in Nazareth some 80 miles away? The Roman Emperor Augustus Caesar solved the "problem" by deciding at this very time to have a census which involved all the people of the Roman Empire going to their birth places for registration. Great movements of all kinds of people of various nationalities would be criss-crossing the Roman World with all sorts of transport or none. Joseph, therefore, migrates from Nazareth to Bethlehem the prophesied birth place of Messiah and the ancestral town of his family, notably King David from whose lineage both Joseph and Mary were descended according to their genealogies in Matthew (Joseph) and Luke (Mary). The chosen pair arrived just at the time Mary was due to deliver her son. The whole world turned upside down for this one special birth!

That there was no place given to the expectant couple is all the more remarkable in that when Mary commences labour she is still left in the outside part of *"the inn"*. We would think that the people there would have been more humanitarian in thought considering her circumstances but especially since they would be of their own kith and kin. As Mary is described in Luke 2 verse 5 as Joseph's *"betrothed wife"*, were they despised and shunned in the unbelief of their relatives? How judgmentally wrong we can be at times! Or perhaps Mary was taken little notice of, being, according to tradition, quite young?

The contrast between the joy at the birth of John Baptist by neighbours and friends and the atmosphere of almost loneliness at the birth of the Lord of Heaven is suggested in the text. In Luke 2 verse 7, Mary seems to be doing everything. *She* brings the child forth and there seems to be no midwife or attendant, *she* wraps Him up and *she* lays Him in the manger. As she was promised a safe pregnancy, so she was promised a safe delivery (Luke 1:35). It is one thing to conceive, another to have a safe delivery of the child. The most dangerous time in a person's life is the 30 minutes or so before birth.[32]

Swaddling bands must have been brought by Mary to Bethlehem for the birth. According to Professor Barclay,[33] they consisted of a square cloth with a long bandage strip coming off one corner. The baby was wrapped in the square first then in the bandage wound around him. This would keep the baby feeling secure and be a source of warmth in the cold Israeli nights.

A manger, the *"Moses basket"* of the Saviour, was the feeding trough of animals. Was it wood or stone? Probably it was the latter. At any rate, it would be clean. No mother would allow otherwise. For a baby to be laid in a manger was to say the least unusual, if not indeed humiliating, but this was a special sign to the shepherds of Bethlehem that this babe was the Saviour of the world.[34] He was born the Saviour, not just to become the Saviour. (He was also known as the King of the Jews to the wise men, not to become the King of the Jews.)

- His conception and birth by a virgin was also a sign to the house of David,[35] as to His true identity. How ironic that present members of the house of David were indeed present at the place of His birth and did not recognise the sign!
- His holy presence in a sinful world was a sign that His name would be *"spoken against"*[36] and how is that sign fulfilled today in the blasphemy of His holy name!
- His death and resurrection was a sign[37] to His generation that He was Messiah in that He was the anti-type of the prophet Jonah.
- Before His coming again there will be signs in the heavens,[38] indicating that He is the Son of Man.

If no human supported the family during His birth, the shepherds were sent by God to cheer the family after the birth and to broadcast this cosmic event. Interestingly, these may have been special shepherds attending the temple flock since Bethlehem is only 9 miles from Jerusalem. Thus they were sent to welcome the Lamb of God, the Shepherd of Israel.

It was a night scene but the glory of the Lord illumined the darkness. Was this the Shekinah glory[39] returning for this momentous event?

What Bethlehem ignored, heaven magnified,[40] with multitudinous rapture and praise. Caesar may no doubt have wished the birth registered on earth in his census but this birth was registered in heaven and published in the news of heaven and earth.[41]

Mary, a mother, with a simple lifestyle, must have been overwhelmed by the natural and supernatural events but remained quiet and dignified throughout. Costly material gifts of gold, frankincense and myrrh, which would be put to good use no doubt after the flight into Egypt, had yet to come with the wise men from the East. The shepherds` visit and the news of heaven`s rejoicing at the birth of her son along with previous personal statement of His future earthly greatness,[42] and blessing to men of goodwill,[43] made her meditate on the faithfulness of God.[44]

She stored *these* "gifts" in the treasury of her heart and they would be there for inward strength when she would suffer the future piercing of the prophesied sword of sorrow[45] when later standing with John at the crucifixion of her Son.

But she would again magnify the Lord, not by herself this time, but with the Apostles and other disciples, other women, and the half -brothers of Jesus in the Upper Room after the Lord`s resurrection.[46] She is now in prayer with them all - not above them all - to God her Saviour.

[29]The definite article is employed in the Septuagint Version of the Old Testament thus distinguishing the meaning of the Greek word *"parthenos"* which can mean a young girl also. The Hebrew word for virgin *"almah"* is also used for a young girl of marriageable years with an unblemished reputation. Objection has been raised that a more specific word for virgin – *"bethulah"* - is not used. But, had this word been used by the prophet it would not have had the immediate application to the wife of King Ahaz. A word with dual application was, therefore, chosen under Divine inspiration.

[30]Vine W.E. *"Expository Dictionary"*, pages 110 and 1240

[31]Hendriksen William *"New Testament Commentary - Luke"*, Banner of Truth, page 938

[32]Rachel did not have a safe delivery. Benjamin was safe but his mother died, probably due to obstructed labour Genesis 35:16-18

[33]Barclay, W. *'The Gospel of Luke'* The New Daily Study Bible, St Andrew Press, Edinburgh , page 26

[34]Luke 2:11

[35]Isaiah 7:13-14

[36]Luke 2:34

[37]Luke 11:30

[38]Luke 21:25-27

[39]The uncreated light of the glory of the Divine presence in the sanctuary as per Exodus 40:34,35

[40]Luke 2:13

[41]Luke 2:14; 17

[42]Luke 1:32

[43]Luke 2:14

[44]Luke 2:19

[45]Luke 2:35

[46]Acts 1:14

The Case of the Great Fever
(Simon's wife's mother, sick with a high fever)

"Now He arose from the synagogue and entered Simon's house. But Simon's wife's mother was sick with a high fever, and they made request of Him concerning her. So He stood over her and rebuked the fever, and it left her. And immediately she arose and served them. When the sun was setting, all those who had any that were sick with various diseases brought them to Him; and He laid His hands on every one of them and healed them. And demons also came out of many, crying out and saying, 'You are the Christ, the Son of God!' And He, rebuking them, did not allow them to speak, for they knew that He was the Christ."

Luke 4 verses 38-41

"Now as soon as they had come out of the synagogue, they entered the house of Simon and Andrew, with James and John. But Simon's wife's mother lay sick with a fever, and they told Him about her at once. So He came and took her by the hand and lifted her up, and immediately the fever left her. And she served them. At evening, when the sun had set, they brought to Him all who were sick and those who were demon-possessed. And the whole city was gathered together at the door. Then He healed many who were sick with various diseases, and cast out many demons; and He did not allow the demons to speak, because they knew Him."

Mark 1 verses 29-34

27

"Now when Jesus had come into Peter's house, He saw his wife's mother lying sick with a fever. So He touched her hand, and the fever left her. And she arose and served them. When evening had come, they brought to Him many who were demon-possessed. And He cast out the spirits with a word, and healed all who were sick, that it might be fulfilled which was spoken by Isaiah the prophet, saying: 'He Himself took our infirmities and bore our sicknesses'."

Matthew 8 verses 14-17

What a contrast from the previously-recorded scene in the Gospels of the Synagogue at Capernaum! There was a man present there with an unclean spirit which the Lord immediately cast out. Imagine having someone with an unclean spirit in your Church! It can and does happen! The Lord`s first miracle in Mark was to cleanse His local Synagogue. His first public duty at Jerusalem as recorded in John was to cleanse the Temple. *"Holiness becomes Thy house, O Lord, for ever."* (Psalm 93:5).

In both cases there was resistance, first in Mark by the unclean spirit; in John by the merchants who made profit from religion. In both cases, Divine authority in action was required and executed. Regarding the latter, we have observed Russian women queuing up in the Church of the Holy Sepulchre in Jerusalem, handing money to an Orthodox priest before being allowed into the supposed site of Calvary to pray; how this must displease the Saviour. *"For by grace are ye saved through faith; and that not of yourselves: it is the GIFT OF GOD, not of works ..."* (Ephesians 2:8).

The scene before us now is a woman with a raging temperature in a house. Not any house, for this was the home of the disciples Simon and Andrew in Capernaum. She is none other than Simon Peter`s mother-in-law. Today there is a Franciscan church built over the reputed site of the house. If correct in location and size it was not a large house.

Disease was rampant in Palestine when "Dr Torrance of Tiberias" went from Scotland to do Missionary service there in 1884. As far as we know, he was the first Christian Missionary doctor to go there since the time of the Lord Jesus. Certain diseases he found were probably similar to those present at the time of our Lord. The Gospel records show the many and varied types of conditions that Jesus dealt with when here on earth.

"Malarial fevers and dysentery were the commonest ailments; of infectious diseases there were no trace at that time," reports Torrance[47] on his arrival in the Holy Land. *"It will be a sad day when any of them make their appearance."* He also tells of the presence of *"a virulent form of malaria"*.

Herbert Lockyer writes: *"Fevers, generated at the marsh land of Tabgha* (near Capernaum) *were common in spring time when this miracle took place"*.[48] Marsh land is where mosquitos would breed so there is a reasonable possibility the great fever was produced by what we now know as malaria since the disease is transmitted by mosquitos. Very high temperatures are reached with the patient having rigors when the parasites are spilled from inside the red blood cells into the blood stream. On such occasions today the bed the patient is in may shake. One cannot be certain as to the cause of this fever, however. We have not been told, and diseases were not scientifically categorised as today. But it fits well with malaria.

According to Galen, the Greek Physician, the ancient Physicians described all fevers as *"Great or small"*. Celsus (25-50 AD) wrote considerably on fevers in *"De Medicina"* Book 111.31 and classified them as Quotidian, tertian and quartan. This fever is described by Dr. Luke as: *"A great fever"*.

The four new disciples brought the Master home from the synagogue to Peter and Andrew`s house after the Sabbath service. Was this fever present before their attendance at the Synagogue and she was now suffering a crisis? If she was so ill before, Peter would surely have remained at home to help.

However, Jesus was asked to come and take control of the situation. He stood over the patient who was seized with, or hard pressed by (Greek – *'sunechomene'*) the fever, assuming the posture of one in command, confronting the disease. *The Lord* would know the origin of the condition. Luke only of the synoptic writers adds the detail of the method of treatment adopted by Jesus in banishing the fever. Hobart comments[49]: "The Lord *'rebuked the fever* and it left her'* at His word"; this expression he says, *"would more naturally come from a medical writer than another"*. Her temperature was suddenly normal again and her strength was immediately restored. Mark narrates that it was before the fever left her that Jesus took her by the hand and lifted her up (Mark 1:31). Indeed, Matthew says that Jesus *"touched her hand, and the fever left her"* (Matthew 8:15). No concern of possible contagion whatever the cause. No recovery time was required. Luke notes that she rose immediately in her restored strength and was fit and willing to serve the assembled company. This would consist of at least six! The Lord, James and John, Peter and Andrew, Peter's wife and his mother-in-law,[50] perhaps more.

His word was the medicine used - a rebuke! The authority of the Great Physician is evident. His word is power. The Lord rebuked the evil spirit in the synagogue; the wind and waves on Galilee's sea and the disciples in Luke 9 verse 55 when they wished to destroy the Samaritans in a village by calling fire to come down from heaven. Whether spirit, nature or disciples, He has the right to and power of rebuke. He is Lord of all. Sometimes we need rebuke, no one is perfect. It is how we react to it that is important.

It was good that Peter sought help for his mother-in-law! Now he is being served by her with the others and can probably expect this favour again when at home in the future. The Physician, however, is now being ministered to immediately by His former patient; most unusual, indeed unique, and this did not escape the attention of the synoptic writers, especially Luke the Physician.

In the calming of the storm, the Lord rebuked the wind first, the cause of the angry sea. The cause was dealt with before the effect. In this case, the Lord reversed that order. He rebuked the symptom first - the fever, the cause disappeared! A Physician would never and could never attempt this order of healing. After diagnosis, he would treat the cause first and the symptoms would then resolve. The heavenly Physician is not bound by laws of Medical Science. He has the liberty to follow, reverse or transcend medical order.

The Sabbath day now ended, the townspeople brought their sick in all its variety to the door of the house. It was now the local Doctor's surgery, indeed local Hospital! A free Health Service was being provided; a politician's dream! Luke points out the Lord treated each in a personal way by laying hands on each individual. This would be irrespective of the duration or virulence of the disease. It has been suggested by W.K. Hobart again[51] that the same mode of treatment was used for them all i.e. laying on of His hands; the same mode perhaps, but not the same treatment for all conditions. Every patient deserved a private consultation and the Lord appreciated each individual`s unique personality and symptom manifestation: the art of Medicine as well as the science.

However, not so the demon-possessed, they were never touched by the Lord Jesus. Demons were cast out by His command.

Matthew says: *"He healed all that were sick"*.[52] Not an unhealthy person left in Capernaum: quite a thought. Local doctors and nurses and paramedics can take a long holiday! However, the people have not only seen but benefitted greatly from *"His mighty works,"* so were deservedly castigated by His woes later on[53] because of their failure to repent of their sins. Great privilege brings great responsibility, a lesson for us all.

Fever is described by Adar Habershon[54] as typical of the restlessness and contagion of sin. Christ gives peace.

As noted earlier, Matthew relates these events to Isaiah 53 verse 4: *"Himself took our infirmities and bare our sicknesses"*. This reveals that Jesus was personal Physician to and for the whole Nation. His practice was not just Capernaum His own city but the whole of Israel.

Also, as previously mentioned, a further and fuller fulfilment would be accomplished by His death at the cross where He personally took upon Himself the sin of the world, thus dealing with the root cause of all disease and sin, not just symptoms. *"With His stripes, we are healed"* (Isaiah 53:5).

---

[47]Livingstone W.P. "*A Galilee Doctor*, The career of Dr D.W. Torrance of Tiberias", Hodder and Stoughton, page 57

[48]H Lockyer '*All the Miracles of the Bible*' at page 171

[49]Hobart W.K. '*The Medical Language of St Luke*', Baker Book House, Michigan 1954, page 4

[50]Mark 1:29

[51]Hobart, *supra*, page 5

[52]Matthew 8:16

[53]Matthew 11:23

[54]Habershon Adar '*The Study of Types*', Kregel Publications, page 79

The Case of the Incurable Disease
(The man with leprosy)

"And it happened when He was in a certain city, that behold, a man who was full of leprosy saw Jesus; and he fell on his face and implored Him, saying, 'Lord, if You are willing, You can make me clean'. Then He put out His hand and touched him, saying, 'I am willing; be cleansed'. Immediately the leprosy left him. And He charged him to tell no one, 'But go and show yourself to the priest, and make an offering for your cleansing, as a testimony to them, just as Moses commanded'. However, the report went around concerning Him all the more; and great multitudes came together to hear, and to be healed by Him of their infirmities. So He Himself often withdrew into the wilderness and prayed."

Luke 5 verses 12-16

"When He had come down from the mountain, great multitudes followed Him. And behold, a leper came and worshiped Him, saying, 'Lord, if You are willing, You can make me clean'. Then Jesus put out His hand and touched him, saying, 'I am willing; be cleansed'. Immediately his leprosy was cleansed. And Jesus said to him, 'See that you tell no one; but go your way, show yourself to the priest, and offer the gift that Moses commanded, as a testimony to them'."

Matthew 8 verses 1-4

"Now a leper came to Him, imploring Him, kneeling down to Him and saying to Him, 'If You are willing, You can make me clean'. Then Jesus, moved with compassion, stretched out His hand

and touched him, and said to him, 'I am willing; be cleansed'. As soon as He had spoken, immediately the leprosy left him, and he was cleansed. And He strictly warned him and sent him away at once, and said to him, 'See that you say nothing to anyone; but go your way, show yourself to the priest, and offer for your cleansing those things which Moses commanded, as a testimony to them'. However, he went out and began to proclaim it freely, and to spread the matter, so that Jesus could no longer openly enter the city, but was outside in deserted places; and they came to Him from every direction."

Mark 1 verses 40-45

Leprosy[55] was looked upon in Old Testament times as a judgment from God. King Uzziah was stricken with leprosy as a judgment for entering the Temple (2 Chronicles 26), an office reserved for the priests.[56] Gehazi was stricken with leprosy for his covetousness in pursuing Naaman the Syrian General for a reward on his recovery from the disease (2 Kings 5). Salvation is free.

"Tsaraath" the Hebrew word for leprosy means 'to strike suddenly'. It was a vile and incurable disease which began so suddenly and unobtrusively, with a painless, usually white spot, gradually spreading throughout the body causing loss of function, sensation and disfigurement. There was no cure, the prospect was death.

In ancient Israel the diagnosis of leprosy lay with the priest. This is seen from Leviticus 13 and 14. He could diagnose, distinguish between types, make prognosis and estimate recovery time. He also took measures of isolation, quarantine, and certification of recovery. In addition, he was to witness the Law of the Leper being performed on the patient's recovery. The leper was not allowed to eat of the holy offerings according to Leviticus 22 verse 4 until cleansed.

It seems clear from Leviticus that some types of 'leprosy' were, however, skin diseases such as psoriasis, eczema or fungal infections. 'Leprosy' in a house, furniture and clothes were obviously due to a mould which if left alone could cause respiratory conditions in the occupants such as aspergillosis or asthma, in addition to any material household damage.

Leprosy in the time of the Greek Physician Hippocrates (460-375 BC) was said[57] to denote skin conditions characterised by scaling. It was separated by him into three different types and this may have still been so in the time of the Lord Jesus. However, it is obvious that this man in Luke 5 had a form of *true leprosy* which was indeed severe. He was *"full of leprosy"* according to Luke the Physician (Luke 5 v 12). That is, an advanced case - he was slowly dying.

He would be grossly disfigured and was somewhat forward in approaching anyone considering his condition as "true Leprosy" which at that time was probably infectious. Even more so as it is just possible the Lord may have been indoors at the time (Mark 1 verse 43 and verse 45) as it says: The Lord *"sent him away (literally, cast him out) ... and he went out (having gone out)"*.

He really had "chutzpah" in approaching the popular Rabbi from Nazareth, considering the instructions given in the Law to separate from society, cover the lips, and cry: *"Unclean!"* (This is how Isaiah felt in the presence of the enthroned pre-incarnate Lord in chapter 6 of his book - like an unclean leper.) Also, any Rabbi would have recoiled in disgust and indignation at the approach of a leper. However, necessity broke convention and shame, perhaps even guilt, if he considered his disease to be the judgment of God upon himself. Albeit, his action showed his faith in Jesus was great, greater than the Law`s restrictions and any personal inhibitions. He was desperate for help. What remarkable trust he had in Jesus` ability considering he had never heard of a leper being cleansed or seen a leper cleansed. He was a pioneer patient but never ever considered himself a guinea pig.

Leprosy is mentioned 68 times in the Bible, 55 in the Old

Testament and 13 in the New Testament yet there is no record of any genuine lepers being cleansed among the Children of Israel under Law in the Old Testament[58] in spite of all the rules and ritual for the cleansing of the leper. Cleansing of the Leper in Jewish society seems to have been reserved as a sign that Messiah had come (Luke 7:22); hence the cleansing of this man now by the Lord Jesus was proof of His presence in the Nation.

The only person reported cleansed in Israel was a Gentile, the Syrian general Naaman (2 Kings 5). The reference by Jesus in His initial address to His local congregation in the synagogue at Nazareth in Luke 4 verse 27 to the cleansing of Naaman the Syrian when there were many lepers in Israel not healed enraged the audience. Grace had gone out to a Gentile and would do so again. There was no leper in the nation of Israel who had faith to be cleansed but now *this* leper had faith in Jesus, Israel`s Messiah and Physician.

His approach was reverent according to the Gospel of Mark 1 verse 40 which says he came "kneeling down". Matthew says in chapter 8 verse 2: "he *worshipped* Him". Thus he may possibly have early recognised the person of Jesus as Divine; Jesus as Messiah and Divine! He *implored* Jesus (Mark 1 verse 40) to cleanse him. The fact that he used the word "cleanse" shows he had insight into the nature of Leprosy according to the Law of Moses. Leprosy is a picture of the *defilement* of sin. He felt unclean, he was defiled. He appealed to the Lord`s will. He believed in His *ability* to cleanse him, the question was - was He *willing* to do so? To touch him would have serious consequences for the Lord Jesus. He would be ceremonially defiled as He was working under the Law.

Jesus had compassion on him, not disgust, revulsion or anger at the illicit approach given the advanced condition of his infectious disease. The synoptic writers all say that Jesus touched him. What a remarkable act! He could have healed him only by His word. Indeed, this is what cleansed him according to Mark 1 verse 41 and

Luke 5 verse 13. But, the touch would convey His identification with him and His compassion. C.S. Lewis says in a letter of 23rd February 1947 that "God chose to be incarnate in a man of delicate sensibilities".

The leper must have been greatly comforted. No one touched lepers for fear of contracting the disease. But this man, Jesus of Nazareth, was different. He was *"Holy, harmless, undefiled and separate from sinners"* (Hebrews 7:26). Instead of contracting illness, He removed it by His power. This was different from the teaching of defilement of the priest in Haggai 2 verses 10-13 through contact. There, the defilement was stronger than the Holy. Here the Holy was stronger than the defilement. The leprosy left him at once, a complete cure having been effected.

It would have been a long time since this man felt human touch. A man liberated from Belsen concentration camp at the end of the Second World War said the human touch was more important than food to those liberated. What a tremendous emotional comfort to him that day as well as total physical healing! There is, according to a New York Professor of Nursing, even a physiological benefit from touch!

The man was not so good at carrying out his instructions as per the *"But"* of Mark 1 verse 45. He had been told emphatically by Jesus to tell no one (verse 44), to report to the priest for religious and civic recognition of the cure and to offer a sacrifice according to the Law of Moses. Jesus was particular that He should be recognised to be working under the Law (Galatians 4:4). In addition, his gift on the eighth day would be offered at the temple and alert functioning priests as to the presence of a Prophet, possibly Messiah, in their midst.

However, the man went about witnessing to his recovery by Jesus, no doubt out of good motive and gratitude for his healing, but in disobedience. The result was an explosion in the popularity of the Lord when He did not want it, leading to growing restriction of His movements, an increased demand for physical healing to the displacement of the priority of preaching of the Kingdom of God, and necessitating His remaining outside populated areas for some time. Thus some other needy people not having easy access to Him could not be ministered to if they were immobile or friendless. Also, Jesus would now be open to the accusation from the religious leaders that he was acting outwith the Law of Moses – "a loose cannon".

Luke now tells us that after this He was - or kept - withdrawing to the wilderness and praying (verse 16). Popularity of the Lord was at peak, always a dangerous time for preachers, teachers or physicians! Now the religious "experts" swarmed in from capital and country to assess Him (verses 17-26) as He was "outside the camp" in their view. He had not studied under any well-known Rabbi in their Theological schools. Who was He?

The teaching of Leviticus 14 being ignored by the leper, "atonement" was not made for him according to the Law. The ritual of this chapter would indicate he was cleansed on the basis of the coming death, burial and resurrection of his Saviour. Thus his failure to attend the priest would indicate that the blood of the sacrificed bird was not applied to the person as prescribed, nor the anointing with oil. Neither would he be presented by the priest before the Lord (Leviticus 14 verse 11). Thus the symbol of Salvation through blood and the sanctified new life in the anointing with oil was not applied; nor his legal acceptance back into society according to the Law.

In Isaiah 53, the nation of Israel is said to have treated the Lord Jesus, God`s Perfect Servant, as a leper in His life and death. In verse 3, He is shunned like a leper would be; in verse 8, He is cut off as a leper, but in verse 10 His days are prolonged as a reinstated leper enjoying the pleasure of the Lord.

Sin, like leprosy, begins small and like leprosy defiles the person and separates him/her from God and others. It silently develops and corrupts the person. Only the Son of God can recover a person from sin and make him/her clean by His shed blood on the cross and keep Him/her clean by the indwelling of the Spirit of God and the continual washing of the water of the Word of God applied to our hearts.

---

[55]Note: E. Carmoly in *"The Occident and American Jewish Advocate"* says "White leprosy" was known from the time of Moses. Manetho (300 BC) records 80,000 Hebrews with "Lepra" in Egypt. Dr Ernest L.McEwan, Rush Medical College, Chicago – *"Leprosy of the Bible in its Medical Aspect"* - pages 195, 196: "At the time of Jesus, *'Lepra graecorum'* denoted a scaly skin condition, *'elephantiasis graecorum'* was true leprosy". The name was later included by the Greeks in the term *'Lepra-Leprosy'*. (Elephantiasis as is known today has no connection.)

[56]The function of the offices of Kingship and Priesthood would only be united - with that of Prophet - in Messiah.

[57]Hippocrates of Cos 460-375 BC in *"Corpus Hipperaticum"* shows the value of Diagnosis and Prognosis and the value of comfort to patients as reported in *"Epidemics"*. This would probably have been known to Luke from the study of Greek Medicine.

[58]There was the leprous hand of Moses as a specific sign of his calling to serve (Exodus 4:6 &7) an indication to him of sin in the heart. There was the leprous condition of Miriam in Numbers 12, as a temporary judgment, but none since under Law.

The Emergency Case -
Healing at a Distance
(The certain centurion's sick servant, ready to die)

"Now when He concluded all His sayings in the hearing of the people, He entered Capernaum. And a certain centurion's servant, who was dear to him, was sick and ready to die. So when he heard about Jesus, he sent elders of the Jews to Him, pleading with Him to come and heal his servant. And when they came to Jesus, they begged Him earnestly, saying that the one for whom He should do this was deserving, 'for he loves our nation, and has built us a synagogue'. Then Jesus went with them. And when He was already not far from the house, the centurion sent friends to Him, saying to Him, 'Lord, do not trouble Yourself, for I am not worthy that You should enter under my roof. Therefore I did not even think myself worthy to come to You. But say the word, and my servant will be healed. For I also am a man placed under authority, having soldiers under me. And I say to one, "Go," and he goes; and to another, "Come," and he comes; and to my servant, "Do this," and he does it.' When Jesus heard these things, He marvelled at him, and turned around and said to the crowd that followed Him, 'I say to you, I have not found such great faith, not even in Israel!' And those who were sent, returning to the house, found the servant well who had been sick."

Luke 7 verses 1-10

"Now when Jesus had entered Capernaum, a centurion came to Him, pleading with Him, saying, 'Lord, my servant is lying at

home paralyzed, dreadfully tormented'. And Jesus said to him, 'I will come and heal him'. The centurion answered and said, 'Lord, I am not worthy that You should come under my roof. But only speak a word, and my servant will be healed. For I also am a man under authority, having soldiers under me. And I say to this one, "Go," and he goes; and to another, "Come," and he comes; and to my servant, "Do this," and he does it.' When Jesus heard it, He marvelled, and said to those who followed, 'Assuredly, I say to you, I have not found such great faith, not even in Israel! And I say to you that many will come from east and west, and sit down with Abraham, Isaac, and Jacob in the kingdom of heaven. But the sons of the kingdom will be cast out into outer darkness. There will be weeping and gnashing of teeth.' Then Jesus said to the centurion, 'Go your way; and as you have believed, so let it be done for you'. And his servant was healed that same hour."

Matthew 8 verses 5-13

Capernaum, a coastal town on the North West of the Sea of Galilee lay on the border of the land allocated by Joshua to Zebulun and Naphtali. Historically, the region was favoured with the blessing of Moses. In Deuteronomy 33 verses 18 and 19 he prophesied Zebulun with Issachar would: "*Partake of the abundance of the seas and of the treasures hidden in the sand*". Naphtali would be: "*Satisfied with favour and full of the blessing of the Lord*" (verse 23). Also, the prophecy of Isaiah 9 verses 1 and 2 was fulfilled in this locality as pointed out in Matthew 4 verses 15 and 16. The people who lived there in darkness certainly saw a great light in the coming of Jesus to Nazareth and Galilee enjoyed God`s special favour as the firstfruits of His ministry. Politically, it was in Herod Antipas` region. Geographically, it was two and a half miles from where the Jordan River entered the Sea of Galilee. Commercially, it was situated on the "Way of the Sea", the great trade route from Damascus to Egypt and was a customs station. Spices and silks were traded there.

There were said to be 4,000 different ships on the Sea of Galilee, mainly fishing vessels, and Capernaum was one of the busy fishing towns. Fruit from the fertile Galilee plains and the fish from the many ports were traded there. It had a strong military presence as well and the Roman Centurion of this passage of Scripture lived there, probably to enforce the *Pax Romana*, albeit in the service of Herod Antipas. It was where Jesus found Matthew *"sitting at the receipt of custom"* and Peter lived there with his wife and mother-in-law.

It was probably named after Nahum the prophet as "Kefar-Nahum", the village of Nahum, and was the base of the Lord`s operations after His exclusion from Nazareth. It is described in Matthew 9 verse 1 as *"His own city"*. It witnessed some of the Lord`s greatest miracles and teaching and was finally cursed by Him for its stubborn unbelief: *"And thou, Capernaum, which art exalted unto heaven, shalt be brought down to hell: for if the mighty works, which have been done in thee, had been done in Sodom, it would have remained until this day. But I say to you, that it will be more tolerable for the land of Sodom in the day of judgment, than for thee"* (Matthew 11:23,24). Today it is a heap of stones and scrub. Great privilege brings great responsibility.

A Roman Centurion was the backbone of the Roman army. The historian Polybius described them as: "Men that can command, steady in action and reliable: ought not to be overanxious to rush into the fight but when pressed, ready to hold their ground and die at their posts".

A dying slave was normally of no import to a Roman citizen, much less to a Centurion. This Centurion, however, had a servant or slave he was fond of and valued. The word used in the original Greek in Matthew`s account of his request in verses 6 and 8 for 'servant' could be used for a young son - *'pais'*, revealing his special regard for him as a father would for a son, although a slave. It is interesting that in the *illustration* of authority in verse 9 the usual word for a slave is used by the Centurion – '*doulos*'. In Luke 7 verse 3, when the elders of the Jews approach Jesus, the word '*doulos*' is used, their view of a slave, but when the Centurion himself speaks in verse 7, he uses the word '*pais*'; his personal regard for his servant. I wonder in fact if the Centurion had adopted him. The use of '*doulos*' in verse 10 is used by the elders of the Jews who had been sent. Again, that is the public view of the servant. It is noteworthy that '*pais*' is the word used in the Septuagint, (the Greek version of the Old Testament) for God`s perfect Servant in Isaiah`s Servant Songs, that Servant being His Son.

It is a moot point whether Matthew may have known this centurion and his home circumstances since his work was based in Capernaum! After all, there was a military presence there and before he was called by Jesus, he was a collector of taxes for the Romans.

This is a very upsetting and serious case. The servant is dying, paralysed and in severe pain ("*in terrific suffering*" NIV). No wonder the Centurion was greatly concerned. It may have been a sudden and severe accident as the word '*bebletai*' translated "lieth" in the AV or "is lying" in the NKJV is literally: "has been thrown down," a perfect passive tense of the Greek word '*ballo*' –to throw, and, as a result, he is now paralysed.

This centurion was in good terms with the local Jewish community as he had built them their synagogue. This was an unusual situation in that the presence of a Roman centurion would normally remind the Jews that they were a conquered nation and produce great resentment and in some cases violence by the Zealots.

He approached the town elders, the local 'toon council' to implore Jesus to come and heal his servant. He thought that they being Jewish officials would have more leverage with Jesus the Jewish Rabbi since he was a Gentile. They did approach the Lord Jesus, continually urging Him to act, in that he deserved His favour for his generosity and his love for the Jewish people. The expression "Built *the* synagogue for us", in verse 5, suggests that a specific synagogue is meant and that he himself built it, probably at no cost to the Jews! Very likely the one Jesus attended, as well as themselves! The present ruins of the limestone synagogue at Capernaum are said to date from the 3rd Century and built on the exact spot and about the same size as the original one made of basalt stone which the Centurion built.

Jesus agreed to their request and started off for his house. It was unusual for a Rabbi to enter a Gentile's house as it rendered him ceremonially unclean. Jesus was showing great grace. However, friends of the Centurion came with the urgent request from him to: *"Just speak a word, and my servant will be healed"* (Luke 7:7)! The Centurion considered that neither he nor his house was good enough (according to Jewish Law) for the Lord's presence and he held Him in such high esteem that[59] he esteemed himself to be unworthy morally, religiously and spiritually to come to Jesus himself. His reason for this conclusion was based on his belief in the power of Christ's word on the principle of authority, something he was familiar with.

His reasoning is military and seems to be as follows: he was a Centurion and as such had a hundred soldiers or so under him. He could command them to do his will because he himself was under authority, the authority of his commander, Caesar. He had authority because *he* was under authority. Jesus had His authority because *He also* was under authority, the authority of God, the God of the Jews, the supreme Authority. Hence He could command and His will would be done. The Lord Jesus could, therefore, heal his servant at one command.

Was he thinking of angelic beings under the command of the Lord Jesus to enact the cure, as some suggest? Not at all. He had faith in the distant efficacy of the spoken word of Jesus. "He recognised the unlimited side of the Lord," says Watchman Nee.[60] Let the Lord Jesus just say a word and healing would be accomplished by the power of His command, even at a distance, any distance. Masterly logic from a concept he was familiar with. He would have gained a "first" at any university! The Lord was astonished at his faith however; no mention of his logic. He turned around and declared He had never seen such faith, not even in His own Nation Israel. This man was a one-off!

The faith of the four (or five) recorded in Mark 2 verse 5; Matthew 9 verse 2; Luke 5 verse 20 met with a response from Jesus but *they* brought the paralysed man in that Scripture to Him. Here, Jesus was being brought initially to the paralysed man.

The servant was healed the very moment the Lord spoke. This was confirmed by the later discussion between the Centurion and the servants at their return to his house. Their watches were cross checked! Healing by Jesus without His physical presence was immediate, just as immediate as would have occurred in His presence!

There is a similar healing at a distance recorded in John 4 verses 46-54 which some have confused with the above. The miracle in John 4 is performed for a Courtier`s son, not a Centurion`s servant. The word used for nobleman means one in the employment of a king suggests Professor John Heading.[61] He suggests this may have been Chuzza, Herod`s steward whose wife Joanna was one of the women who ministered to the Lord.

The miracle on the Courtier`s son is done in Cana of Galilee not Capernaum. The servant whose story is recorded in Luke and Matthew was paralysed and in pain. The son of the Courtier in John had a fever. In Luke, Jesus goes part of the way to the house in Capernaum. In John, He heals from Cana of Galilee with the effect in Capernaum, an even greater distance! In both, however, it is the naked word of Jesus that is believed with effect.

Jesus, the Great Physician, shows in these two miracles His ability to heal immediately at a distance by His word with an absent patient He has never seen!! No physician other than Jesus could or can do this. Their training is to observe, question, examine, investigate, diagnose, instigate treatment and suggest outcome.

The wonder of healing at a distance is truly amazing. But surely the concept of this Centurion is the basis of believing prayer. We have an almighty God who is *"Over all ... blessed forever"* (Romans 9:5) and He has given us command of access to Him through the name of Jesus. We have today an even greater distance physically, from Earth to Heaven, but we reach God in prayer faster than the speed of light!

How amazing, therefore, the words of Isaiah 45 verse 11: *"Ask Me of things to come concerning My sons, and concerning the work of My hands command ye Me!"*

---

[59]Edersheim Alfred, *"The Life and Times of Jesus the Messiah"*, Longmans, Green, and Co. 1900 vol.1, page 548

[60]Nee Watchman, *"The Glory of His Life"*, Christian Fellowship Publications, page 101

[61]Heading J. *"John - What the Bible Teaches"*, John Ritchie, Kilmarnock, Scotland, page 83

The Orthopaedic Case
(The ambulance with the paralysed man)

"Now it happened on a certain day, as He was teaching, that there were Pharisees and teachers of the law sitting by, who had come out of every town of Galilee, Judea, and Jerusalem. And the power of the Lord was present to heal them. Then behold, men brought on a bed a man who was paralyzed, whom they sought to bring in and lay before Him. And when they could not find how they might bring him in, because of the crowd, they went up on the housetop and let him down with his bed through the tiling into the midst before Jesus. When He saw their faith, He said to him, 'Man, your sins are forgiven you'. And the scribes and the Pharisees began to reason, saying, 'Who is this who speaks blasphemies? Who can forgive sins but God alone?' But when Jesus perceived their thoughts, He answered and said to them, 'Why are you reasoning in your hearts? Which is easier, to say, "Your sins are forgiven you," or to say, "Rise up and walk"? But that you may know that the Son of Man has power on earth to forgive sins' — He said to the man who was paralyzed, 'I say to you, arise, take up your bed, and go to your house'. Immediately he rose up before them, took up what he had been lying on, and departed to his own house, glorifying God. And they were all amazed, and they glorified God and were filled with fear, saying, 'We have seen strange things today!'"

Luke 5 verses 17-26

"And again He entered Capernaum after some days, and it was heard that He was in the house. Immediately many gathered together, so that there was no longer room to receive them, not

even near the door. And He preached the word to them. Then they came to Him, bringing a paralytic who was carried by four men. And when they could not come near Him because of the crowd, they uncovered the roof where He was. So when they had broken through, they let down the bed on which the paralytic was lying. When Jesus saw their faith, He said to the paralytic, 'Son, your sins are forgiven you'. And some of the scribes were sitting there and reasoning in their hearts, 'Why does this Man speak blasphemies like this? Who can forgive sins but God alone?' But immediately, when Jesus perceived in His spirit that they reasoned thus within themselves, He said to them, 'Why do you reason about these things in your hearts? Which is easier, to say to the paralytic, "Your sins are forgiven you," or to say, "Arise, take up your bed and walk"? But that you may know that the Son of Man has power on earth to forgive sins' —He said to the paralytic, 'I say to you, arise, take up your bed, and go to your house'. Immediately he arose, took up the bed, and went out in the presence of them all, so that all were amazed and glorified God, saying, 'We never saw anything like this!'"

Mark 2 verses 1-12

"So He got into a boat, crossed over, and came to His own city. Then behold, they brought to Him a paralytic lying on a bed. When Jesus saw their faith, He said to the paralytic, 'Son, be of good cheer; your sins are forgiven you'. And at once some of the scribes said within themselves, 'This Man blasphemes!' But Jesus, knowing their thoughts, said, 'Why do you think evil in your hearts? For which is easier, to say, "Your sins are forgiven you," or to say, "Arise and walk"? But that you may know that the Son of Man has power on earth to forgive sins' —then He said to the paralytic, 'Arise, take up your bed, and go to your house'. And he arose and departed to his house. Now when the multitudes saw it, they marveled and glorified God, who had given such power to men."

Matthew 9 verses 1-8

How this man came to be paralysed we do not know. But, a Physician or Surgeon would want to know as it is crucial to diagnosis and treatment. Was it from birth? Was it the result of an accident? Was it a stroke? Was it a long-term neurological illness? We do not know but the perf. passive participle used by Luke of *"paralysed"* in verse 18 and the form of the construction, as well as indicating the permanence of the paralysis may perhaps suggest a more recent event. Robert Young in his *"Literal Translation of the Bible"* says: *"A man who hath been struck with palsy"*. The fact that he had four friends or relatives immediately performing as an ambulance and carrying him to where Jesus was could suggest a more recent occurrence. Long-term illness does not often awaken such enthusiasm and faith in friends and relatives! The man paralysed for 38 years in John 9 had no one to help him. We are not specifically told if this was a recent event or not. Howbeit an efficient and emergency ambulance was at hand. Traffic lights would be no obstacle to these men!

Why four people? Was this a heavy man? Was the distance to the house where Jesus was staying far away? Or was the man in pain with the paralysis and four ambulance men were needed to cushion his limbs while transporting him to Jesus?

Interestingly the ESV translation of the Bible translates Mark 2 verse 1 as Jesus being *"At home"*, so was this the Lord`s own rented accommodation, or the house of Peter and Andrew who lived in Capernaum? This brings a new focus on the subsequent repair of the roof!

Jewish thought at the time connected illness with sin and indeed in the New Testament there is such a connection made in 1 Corinthians 10 verse 9; Chapter 11 verse 30; James 5 verse 1 and 1 John 5 verse 16, although this is not always the case. Hence Jesus` priority in dealing with the man`s sin before attending to his physical ailment in the presence of such an elite audience of Pharisees and Doctors of the Law already gathered in the house from all over the country.

The ambulance men were persistent and imaginative if a trifle ruthless in their determination to have their friend or brother cured. Their faith along with that of the patient was unquestionable. Whose faith was first in motivating this expedition? The patient's or the porters' or all together?

The problem was the obstacle of a house crowded with people and the inaccessibility of Jesus to them. They came late to Jesus and the difficulties were, therefore, the greater. How true this is in life! The crowd hide Jesus and there are usually difficulties in the way to finding Him which become greater over the course of time. Better and easier to come to the Saviour early and give your life to Him when young.

The solution decided upon was to carry the patient up the outside stairs situated at the side of the house, on to the flat roof and gouge an adequate opening in the surface tiling through which they could lower him on his stretcher bed. On carrying the man up the stairs the two men at the lower end would feel the weight most! The two at the front would guide the procedure. Co-operation and different function required, but unity of purpose, although some shoulder a greater burden! The roof could be fixed later, the Great Physician could fix their patient now. In Luke's account the man was lowered *"Into the midst before Jesus"*. The friends were accurate in their estimate of where exactly Jesus was. Those who lead others to Christ must know Him personally, where to find Him in the Scriptures of truth, the Bible, and how to introduce the person to Him.

Imagine the reaction of the crowd in the house to the scraping and pulling at the tiling of the roof, dust falling on to their upturned heads. 'Vandals!' they would shout; but the four persevere. *"From the days of John the Baptist until now the kingdom of heaven suffers violence, and the violent take it by force"* says the Lord (Matthew 11:12).

First of all, Jesus gave hope. In Matthew's account, Chapter 9 verse 2, He called the paralysed man "*Son*" and told him to "*cheer up!*" The Lord rewarded their perseverance but not in the way they expected. His sins were forgiven first. They had not come about this. Jesus deals with the root before dealing with the fruit of the problem. How much of treatment today is symptomatic instead of radical, e.g. self-help groups, alternative medicine, methadone for drug addiction, etc. A local Christian rehab centre aims to get addicts off drugs in one week and mostly succeeds. The secret is dealing with the root cause - sin. This, of course, is not "politically correct" as it does not fit with a humanistic view of man, but it works because it is in harmony with God's view of man! The immediate power given to this man was obvious and public. He did not need a course of treatment, not even for a week.

The logic in the discussion with the scribes and the Pharisees was that Jesus' claim to do what He said i.e. forgive sins, a spiritual act and unseen, was vindicated in the miraculous and physical act which could be seen. Both were acts of God. Thus He showed He was God in human flesh as only *God* can forgive sins. The trouble was that the religious experts were not open and deep enough in their thinking about God to appreciate the logic of the situation which revealed the Deity of Christ. Perhaps because of tradition, prejudice or blindness, their appreciation of the Lord Jesus was blocked.

It is noteworthy that Jesus could read their thoughts. This is a fulfilment of the prophecy of Simeon in Luke 2 verse 35: "*That the thoughts of many hearts may be revealed*" and is a feature of the Gospel of Luke e.g. Chapter 6 verse 8; 9 verse 47 and 24 verse 38.

It sometimes takes more than one person to interest another in Jesus. Four people focusing on a person's salvation must produce results. As remarked, each had a part to play, two with heavier responsibility, but co-operation achieved the desired result.

One has observed that the man went home carrying what used to carry him. The Lord had power over his sin and paralysis, he now had power over his bed. He was a happy man, he was glorifying God. His sins were forgiven, any pain was gone, his mobility was restored and he could walk normally. What a transformation, inside and out!

The immediate social reaction was one of mixed feelings- amazement, praise and fear. They admitted to seeing "strange things" that day. It was a day for the town to remember. This town now knew the power of Christ both physically and spiritually. How would it respond? We know from later Scriptures.

The personal story ends there in Scripture but not in life. He would now have domestic responsibilities he never had before. He would need to look for work and engage with society. He would need to cope with local "celeb" status for a while. But also perhaps some hostility, he had jumped the queue for attention and was the cause of a house being wrecked. Not all would be pleased at his cure. Would the men who brought him fix the roof?

The Neurological Case
(The handicapped man)

"Now it happened on another Sabbath, also, that He entered the synagogue and taught. And a man was there whose right hand was withered. So the scribes and Pharisees watched Him closely, whether He would heal on the Sabbath, that they might find an accusation against Him. But He knew their thoughts, and said to the man who had the withered hand, 'Arise and stand here'. And he arose and stood. Then Jesus said to them, 'I will ask you one thing: Is it lawful on the Sabbath to do good or to do evil, to save life or to destroy?' And when He had looked around at them all, He said to the man, 'Stretch out your hand'. And he did so, and his hand was restored as whole as the other. But they were filled with rage, and discussed with one another what they might do to Jesus."

Luke 6 verses 6-11

"And He entered the synagogue again, and a man was there who had a withered hand. So they watched Him closely, whether He would heal him on the Sabbath, so that they might accuse Him. And He said to the man who had the withered hand, 'Step forward'. Then He said to them, 'Is it lawful on the Sabbath to do good or to do evil, to save life or to kill?' But they kept silent. And when He had looked around at them with anger, being grieved by the hardness of their hearts, He said to the man, 'Stretch out your hand'. And he stretched it out, and his hand was restored as whole as the other. Then the Pharisees went out and immediately plotted with the Herodians against Him, how they might destroy Him."

Mark 3 verses 1-6

> *"Now when He had departed from there, He went into their synagogue. And behold, there was a man who had a withered hand. And they asked Him, saying, 'Is it lawful to heal on the Sabbath?' — that they might accuse Him. Then He said to them, 'What man is there among you who has one sheep, and if it falls into a pit on the Sabbath, will not lay hold of it and lift it out? Of how much more value then is a man than a sheep? Therefore it is lawful to do good on the Sabbath.' Then He said to the man, 'Stretch out your hand'. And he stretched it out, and it was restored as whole as the other. Then the Pharisees went out and plotted against Him, how they might destroy Him."*

Matthew 12 verses 9-14

The Man with the withered hand - This man's handicap did not prevent him from attending worship but he could never have been an officiating priest (Leviticus 21:16). His deformity forbad it. The perfect passive tense in Greek in Mark 3 verse 1 would suggest that this was not congenital in origin according to Professor W. Barclay in his commentary on Mark 3.[62] Some accident or illness had interrupted this man's normal life. Whatever the cause, he was not bitter against God regarding his condition. He still attended public worship. It was just as well or he would never have encountered Jesus personally in the synagogue that Sabbath day.

Luke only of the synoptic Gospels observantly notes with the eye of a Physician that it was the right hand that was handicapped, the dominant hand in the majority of people. So he would have had considerable limitations in life. It is noteworthy that being *"withered"* or *"shrivelled"* (NIV), "A word used for dried fruit,"[63] the man must have had this hand condition for some time, perhaps having Volkmann's Ischaemic Contracture,[64] a condition usually resulting from injury to the forearm or hand. An apocryphal story says he was a stone mason. If so he may have suffered an accident at work some time previously which later resulted in his handicap.

Why then did Jesus heal him on the Sabbath knowing his condition was long standing and that it would invoke controversy, indeed hostility, from the Jews? Indeed, they *"kept watching"* (Luke 6 verse 7) Jesus to see if He would heal him in order to accuse Him. Since the case was not life-threatening in received religious orthodoxy, it could wait till the Sabbath was over. But Jesus had publicly established His authority over the Sabbath in the previous verses in the Gospel of Mark from the Holy Scriptures which they said they upheld. Also, the Lord met people in their present need.

Once again Jesus reads the thoughts of the scribes and Pharisees, the second occasion He is recorded as doing so. In the previous verses of the chapter, it was the disciples that the Jews attacked. Now it was the Lord Himself they targeted. He was judged and condemned before He acted.

But, He demonstrated:

- Higher moral and spiritual ground in that doing good was superior to the hardness of their hearts - Mark 3 verses 4 and 5.
- In the Law, the principle of the Sabbath is for the good of man. He is about to do good.
- The Lord challenges their understanding of the Sabbath in Luke 6 verse 9 and Matthew 12 verses 11 and 12, from even a humanitarian principle: *"How much more valuable is a man than sheep"* and applies this in relation to this man`s case.
- As the Lord of the Sabbath (Luke 6 verse 5) He was bringing this man into rest. Was that not the intention of the Sabbath? He was fulfilling the purpose of the Sabbath.[65]

A Physician surely heals on the Sabbath. However, as Norman Crawford points out in his commentary on Luke[66], either a positive or negative answer to the question Jesus asked: *"Is it lawful on the Sabbath to do good or to do evil?"* (Mark 3 verse 4) would have brought self-condemnation on His enemies, therefore it remained unanswered and this filled them with frustration and anger. Jesus may have been a Physician but He disputed here like a Lawyer, an Advocate! *"Stretch out your hand"* the Lord briefly commands and the man immediately obeys and is healed.

This may have been the only opportunity of healing for the man. The Lord was moving on in His ministry and opposition to Him was increasing.

Legality in their thinking came before mercy. Their interpretation of the Law of Moses and human tradition obscured rather than revealed the nature of God and their lack of sense of proper priorities led to this hatred of the Lord Jesus. It would not have been conducive for the Lord to perform this work of mercy when there were so many opposing spirits. We have to take care not to have the spirit and reasoning of the Pharisee and thus hinder the work of God.

This miracle is thought worthy of recording by all three synoptic writers although one may consider it much less significant than some others. Perhaps this is because in this healing the definite shift in the religious establishment's attitude became permanently antagonistic toward Jesus. He was now established in their view as a Lawbreaker and repeated desecrator of the Sabbath. Their prejudice overcame their antipathy towards the Herodians in the formulation of a conspiracy to plot His death.[67] No thought of rethinking and re-examination of *their* view regarding their understanding of the Sabbath was ever considered.

The Lord, therefore, prayed to His father after this in all-night communion (Luke 6:12) and decided to choose 12 men to whom He could commit His ministry after His death.

The man himself never would have expected such a life-changing event as the miraculous healing of his hand on attending the synagogue that day. He took courage and was willing to take a public stand for Jesus before a congregation which knew him when invited to do so and to exercise faith in His word. So he came into blessing. This reminds us of the Billy Graham rallies in Glasgow in 1955, when people (like myself) came forward to receive Christ by faith when publicly invited. What a life-changing decision coming to Jesus Christ makes! He would now forever be associated in the minds of the local people with the person of Jesus and may have to share in His rejection in days to come. He would also now be looking for work; his right hand was normal now!

We so often come from worship healed in spirit after an encounter with the living God and also demonstrate public witness of our association with Him just by simple attendance at the fellowship meetings. *"Do not forget the assembling of ourselves together as the manner of some is, but exhorting one another and so much the more as you see the Day approaching"* (Hebrews 10:25). The Day is approaching - fast!

How was the man healed? He had faith in the Lord when He commanded him to do what he was not able to do naturally. It is interesting to note that the damaged hand was *"restored whole as the other"*. Not a youth`s hand, nor an aged but a new *right* hand, one suited to his age and the same size as the other, a bespoke hand! Nerve repair effected and blood supply fully restored with normal appearance and function.

No one would have guessed that he ever had a useless hand in the past. Is this not how God works in grace. *"He restores that which He takes not away"* (see Psalm 69:4). He would have been very glad he had attended the synagogue that Sabbath and had met the Great Physician.

The man had his right hand restored by Heaven`s *"Benjamin"*, Jesus, the Son of the right hand, who has now been exalted to the right hand of His Father God[68] after being *"Benoni"* Son of sorrow[69] on the cross. He is now Lord of all, not just of the Sabbath.

---

[62]Barclay William, *"The Gospel of Mark"*, New Daily Study Bible, Saint Andrew Press, Edinburgh, page 76

[63]Crawford Norman, *"Luke - What the Bible Teaches"*, John Ritchie Ltd, Kilmarnock, page 102

[64]Volkmann's ischaemic contracture is a claw-like deformity of the hand, fingers and wrist. It occurs as a result of trauma, perhaps a previous fracture. It was originally thought to be due to nerve damage but lack of blood supply is involved in the process resulting in fibrosis and shortening of the flexor forearm muscles.

[65]Farrar F.W., *"The Life of Christ"*, Cassel and Company Ltd., 1884, page 209

[66]Crawford Norman, *"Luke - What the Bible Teaches"*, John Ritchie Ltd., Kilmarnock, page 102

[67]Mark 3 verse 6

[68]Psalm 110 verse 1; Mark 16 verse 19; Hebrews 1 verse 3; etc.

[69]Genesis 35 verse 18

The Psychiatric Case
(The man of Gadara)

"Then they sailed to the country of the Gadarenes, which is opposite Galilee. And when He stepped out on the land, there met Him a certain man from the city who had demons for a long time. And he wore no clothes, nor did he live in a house but in the tombs. When he saw Jesus, he cried out, fell down before Him, and with a loud voice said, 'What have I to do with You, Jesus, Son of the Most High God? I beg You, do not torment me!' For He had commanded the unclean spirit to come out of the man. For it had often seized him, and he was kept under guard, bound with chains and shackles; and he broke the bonds and was driven by the demon into the wilderness. Jesus asked him, saying, 'What is your name?' And he said, 'Legion', because many demons had entered him. And they begged Him that He would not command them to go out into the abyss. Now a herd of many swine was feeding there on the mountain. So they begged Him that He would permit them to enter them. And He permitted them. Then the demons went out of the man and entered the swine, and the herd ran violently down the steep place into the lake and drowned. When those who fed them saw what had happened, they fled and told it in the city and in the country. Then they went out to see what had happened, and came to Jesus, and found the man from whom the demons had departed, sitting at the feet of Jesus, clothed and in his right mind. And they were afraid. They also who had seen it told them by what means he who had been demon-possessed was healed. Then the whole multitude of the surrounding region of the Gadarenes asked Him to depart from them, for they were seized with great fear. And He got into the boat and returned. Now the

man from whom the demons had departed begged Him that he might be with Him. But Jesus sent him away, saying, 'Return to your own house, and tell what great things God has done for you'. And he went his way and proclaimed throughout the whole city what great things Jesus had done for him."

Luke 8 verses 26-39

"Then they came to the other side of the sea, to the country of the Gadarenes. And when He had come out of the boat, immediately there met Him out of the tombs a man with an unclean spirit, who had his dwelling among the tombs; and no one could bind him, not even with chains, because he had often been bound with shackles and chains. And the chains had been pulled apart by him, and the shackles broken in pieces; neither could anyone tame him. And always, night and day, he was in the mountains and in the tombs, crying out and cutting himself with stones. When he saw Jesus from afar, he ran and worshiped Him. And he cried out with a loud voice and said, 'What have I to do with You, Jesus, Son of the Most High God? I implore You by God that You do not torment me'. For He said to him, 'Come out of the man, unclean spirit!' Then He asked him, 'What is your name?' And he answered, saying, 'My name is Legion; for we are many'. Also he begged Him earnestly that He would not send them out of the country. Now a large herd of swine was feeding there near the mountains. So all the demons begged Him, saying, 'Send us to the swine, that we may enter them'. And at once Jesus gave them permission. Then the unclean spirits went out and entered the swine (there were about two thousand); and the herd ran violently down the steep place into the sea, and drowned in the sea. So those who fed the swine fled, and they told it in the city and in the country. And they went out to see what it was that had happened. Then they came to Jesus, and saw the one who had been demon-possessed and had the legion, sitting and clothed and in his right mind. And they were afraid. And those who saw it told them how it happened to him who had been demon-possessed, and about the swine. Then they began to plead with Him to depart from their region. And when He got into the boat, he who had been demon-possessed begged Him that he might be with Him. However, Jesus did not permit him, but said to him, 'Go home to your friends, and tell them what great things the Lord has done for you, and how He has had compassion on you'. And he departed and began to proclaim in Decapolis all that Jesus had done for him; and all marvelled."

Mark 5 verses 1-20

"When He had come to the other side, to the country of the Gergesenes, there met Him two demon-possessed men, coming out of the tombs, exceedingly fierce, so that no one could pass that way. And suddenly they cried out, saying, 'What have we to do with You, Jesus, You Son of God? Have You come here to torment us before the time?' Now a good way off from them there was a herd of many swine feeding. So the demons begged Him, saying, 'If You cast us out, permit us to go away into the herd of swine'. And He said to them, 'Go'. So when they had come out, they went into the herd of swine. And suddenly the whole herd of swine ran violently down the steep place into the sea, and perished in the water. Then those who kept them fled; and they went away into the city and told everything, including what had happened to the demon-possessed men. And behold, the whole city came out to meet Jesus. And when they saw Him, they begged Him to depart from their region."

Matthew 8 verses 28-34

It is very obvious that this man had severe demon possession but it manifested itself in psychiatric and somatic symptoms, hence I have placed it under the term "Psychiatric". There is recognised interaction between spirit, soul and body (see 1 Thessalonians 5:23) and we see here the effect of all three. The Bible clearly distinguishes between lunacy and demon possession in Matthew 4 verse 24.

The Gospel of Matthew mentions two demon possessed men in

the region of Gadara but Luke and Mark concentrate on one called Legion.

The place where the man lived was in the territory of Herod Philip where there was a more lax attitude to Judaic customs. This is seen in the abundance of pigs; an unclean animal to the Jews according to Leviticus 11 verse 7 and Deuteronomy 14 verse 8.

We note the plight of the man first of all bodily. He would be thin physically from his agitated state burning up calories and probable poor diet. He was naked and so his wounds and scars from self-harming were easily seen. His mind was affected in that he was disturbed, in distress, highly emotional, impulsive in behaviour and shouting. His self-harming would certainly not be due to any attention-seeking but to lack of self-esteem, despair, even depersonalisation. It may have relieved emotional tension for a short time but then the habit became repetitive and addictive. It could indeed have led to suicide in the end.

Having left his home, he lived with the stench of death in tombs at night and the wild habitat of the wilderness during the day. A modern view of him could conclude he had a "Multiple Personality Disorder" or "Dissociative Identity Disorder" from the symptoms described. He said a legion of demons possessed him, *"For we are many,"* (a Roman Legion of the time consisted of approximately 5,000 soldiers). His given name was sublimated to the name, "Legion", a collective name. Why this name? Had he suffered abuse by Roman soldiers from a certain legion in the past? We know from John Baptist's statement in Luke 3 verse 14 that they could be violent or oppressive at times. Had abuse allowed the entrance of a host of demons? Or had he become involved with and subsequently captured by the occult? His "personality protection barrier", if one may coin an expression, had become broken down from an unknown cause. *"Whoso breaketh a hedge, a serpent shall bite him."*[70] This can occur today with drug and alcohol abuse, a giving over to certain dark music and invitation of spirits as well as certain types of physical and mental abuse.

The number represented by "legion" is questioned by some, but it is of interest that about 2,000 demons entered the swine (Mark 5:13). The Bible says he was demon-possessed, so we may presume he had *at least* 2,000 demons!

Sometimes the man speaks as in verse 28 of Luke 8; sometimes the demons speak through the man as in verse 9 of Mark 5: "For *we* are many"; sometimes the singular is used as in verse 29 of Luke 8: "He had commanded the unclean *spirit* … for *it* had often seized him …" and sometimes a plurality of spirits speak as in verse 31 of Luke 8: "*They* begged Him that He would not command *them*". It is believed that in such cases there is a lead demon in charge of subordinate spirits.[71] Demons appear to like embodiment.

He was a long time like this, with no hope of recovery. The evil spirits in him empowered him to break every chain. This is the opposite to Samson who in his Nazarite vow could not be bound with cords through the inward power of the Holy Spirit coming upon him.[72] He terrified the neighbourhood, blocked the roads (Matthew 8:28) and people could no longer cope with him. They had tried to contain him by damage limitation of guarded imprisonment with chains on his hands and shackles on his feet to no avail. This is a vivid demonstration of the futility of Laws to radically change a person. No chain could bind him, says Mark 5 verses 3 and 4, and no one was strong enough to subdue him. Science and humanism failed as well. Only the Gospel has the power to set people free and change them. "*It is the power of God unto salvation to everyone who believes*" (Romans 1:16).

The spirits immediately knew who Jesus was. The disciples, as revealed on various occasions did not. "*What manner of man is this?*" they exclaimed, on witnessing the calming of the storm at sea. The religious leaders at Jerusalem - the Pharisees and Sadducees, elders and scribes did not: Herod and Pilate did not, but this man who was demon-possessed did!

The demons knew the Lord Jesus as the Son of the Most High God. Andrew Jukes in his book *"The Names of God"* says, at page 88, that "The name El Elyon (the Most High God) whenever used, its special and distinctive sense is always that the person or thing it speaks of is the highest of a series or order of like natures". He continues on the next page: "even fallen angels, whatever the depth of their fall, are partakers of a nature that is descended from Him".

These demons although created by God, fell from their first estate and associated themselves with the one who said: *"I will ascend above the heights of the clouds, I will be as the Most High"*.[73] They knew their time on earth was limited and that their future doom in the Abyss and final destruction in the Lake of Fire was certain. Meanwhile, they were playing cat and mouse with this poor man.

It is tragic to see that this man, who recognised Jesus, thought He would make him worse! Such was his deluded mind-set. Whoever became worse by trusting and following Jesus? Satan has blinded and warped minds today so that many consider Christ would cramp their personal freedom and spoil their enjoyment of life. It is the Devil`s deception. The Lord Jesus has come to loose us from chains which bind us and that we *"Might have life, and have it to the full"*.[74]

We next observe the might of Jesus: *"For this purpose the Son of God was manifested, that He might destroy the works of the devil"*.[75] He is stronger than Satan: *"A strong man armed keeps his goods in peace but if a stronger than he comes, he overcomes him, takes away his armour wherein he trusts and divides his spoils"*.[76] By His glorious resurrection after His invasion of Satan`s domain in death, He bound him till the time of his final doom.

- Jesus has physical power. We see a glimpse of this in the case of the paralysed man in Mark 2.

- He has psychological power since He knows our thoughts. We have noted this in the Gospel of Luke repeatedly: *"Jesus knowing their thoughts …"*. Indeed, He has unique psychological power, He *understands* our thoughts afar off.[77]

- He has power over nature as seen in His calming of the storm.

- He has power over animal, fish and bird life. He rides an unbroken colt in His entrance as the King into Jerusalem on Palm Sunday[78] and knows where a fish is in the sea with a coin of the exact value required in its mouth[79], the exact time and how often a cock will crow in the city of Jerusalem.[80]

- He has resurrection power: *"I have power to lay down my life and power to take it again"*.[81]

- He has spiritual power as seen here with the demoniac.

- He is the head of all principality and power[82].

- He has *all* power: *"All power is given unto me in Heaven and on earth"*.[83]

The man of Gadara is transformed. He is found seated at the feet of Jesus, clothed and in his right mind. The clothes would cover his former self–inflicted wounds. His past was over and people who did not know him before would never have guessed his past history. He is a new creation in Christ: he is so changed the locals are now frightened by his tranquility!

He is so grateful to his Saviour; he wanted to be near Him, to listen to Him, to follow Him. He is like the Prodigal Son who *"When he came to himself"* returned to his father`s house. He had a new mind. He would be able to think clearly, concentrate, make rational decisions, plan his future life. More importantly, *the spirit* of his mind was transformed by the Holy Spirit. But his request to follow Jesus was forbidden: *"Go home to your own people and tell what great things the Lord has done for you and how He had mercy on you*.[84] His mission was to tell his story to his own people, in his own locality and to all who would listen. The new Spirit within him would empower him.

He could go where Jesus could not, since the Saviour was asked to leave the area. The people were afraid of the presence and power of the Lord Jesus but He was leaving His witness and substitute. This witness he did effectively throughout Decapolis, the Gentile, mainly heathen, cities in Peraea on the East of the Jordan[85]preaching about how much Jesus had done for him. He seemed to have no shame with regard to his former unclothed state and anti-social behaviour. He was a new man. His testimony proved effective and evoked wonder in the population.

It has been asked why Jesus asked this man to testify to Him when He forbad this on the West side of the Sea of Galilee. It has been suggested that this was because in Decapolis there was no danger of the revolutionary excitement which was always likely to break out among the Jews of Galilee.[86]

The gospel is a radical message with immediate and unrestricted power when believed. It is shown here to transform the mind of a severely demon-possessed man. His spirit, soul and body are made whole. It reaches the depths of the human personality.

This man was delivered from strong powers outside and within himself by the all-mighty power of the Lord Jesus, the Son of God.

All this took place in one day. Did the Lord cross the Lake of Galilee with His disciples just to meet this man? I think He did. Jesus has a personal interest in individuals and there is no impossible case with Him. Indeed, He is the specialist of impossible cases.

[70]Ecclesiastes 10 verse 8 AV
[71]Hugh Black, former pastor Struthers Memorial Church, Greenock ipse dixit
[72]Judges 13 verses 5, 25; 16 verse 12
[73]Isaiah 14 verse 14
[74]John 10 verse 10 NIV
[75]1 John 3 verse 8 NKJV
[76]Luke 11 verses 21, 22
[77]Psalm 139 verse 2
[78]Matthew 21 verse 5
[79]Matthew 17 verse 27
[80]Mark 14 verses 30, 72
[81]John 10 verse 18
[82]Colossians 2 verse 10
[83]Matthew 28 verse 18
[84]Mark 5 verse 19
[85]Ten cities of Greek culture, language and religion with their own government. Only Scythopolis (ancient Beth-shean) was on the West side of Jordan. (Edersheim Alfred *"Sketches of Jewish Social Life"*, Updated Edition, page 23.
[86]*"Cambridge Greek Testament for Schools and Colleges"*, Cambridge University Press, 1889, page 89.

The Gynaecological Case
(The woman having a flow of blood for 12 years)

"So it was, when Jesus returned, that the multitude welcomed Him, for they were all waiting for Him. And behold, there came a man named Jairus, and he was a ruler of the synagogue. And he fell down at Jesus' feet and begged Him to come to his house, for he had an only daughter about twelve years of age, and she was dying. But as He went, the multitudes thronged Him. Now a woman, having a flow of blood for twelve years, who had spent all her livelihood on physicians and could not be healed by any, came from behind and touched the border of His garment. And immediately her flow of blood stopped. And Jesus said, "Who touched Me?" When all denied it, Peter and those with him said, 'Master, the multitudes throng and press You, and You say, "'Who touched Me?'" But Jesus said, 'Somebody touched Me, for I perceived power going out from Me'. Now when the woman saw that she was not hidden, she came trembling; and falling down before Him, she declared to Him in the presence of all the people the reason she had touched Him and how she was healed immediately. And He said to her, 'Daughter, be of good cheer; your faith has made you well. Go in peace'. While He was still speaking, someone came from the ruler of the synagogue's house, saying to him, 'Your daughter is dead. Do not trouble the Teacher'. But when Jesus heard it, He answered him, saying, 'Do not be afraid; only believe, and she will be made well'. When He came into the house, He permitted no one to go in except Peter,

James, and John, and the father and mother of the girl. Now all wept and mourned for her; but He said, 'Do not weep; she is not dead, but sleeping'. And they ridiculed Him, knowing that she was dead. But He put them all outside, took her by the hand and called, saying, 'Little girl, arise'. Then her spirit returned, and she arose immediately. And He commanded that she be given something to eat. And her parents were astonished, but He charged them to tell no one what had happened."

Luke 8 verses 40-56

"Now when Jesus had crossed over again by boat to the other side, a great multitude gathered to Him; and He was by the sea. And behold, one of the rulers of the synagogue came, Jairus by name. And when he saw Him, he fell at His feet and begged Him earnestly, saying, 'My little daughter lies at the point of death. Come and lay Your hands on her, that she may be healed, and she will live.' So Jesus went with him, and a great multitude followed Him and thronged Him. Now a certain woman had a flow of blood for twelve years, and had suffered many things from many physicians. She had spent all that she had and was no better, but rather grew worse. When she heard about Jesus, she came behind Him in the crowd and touched His garment. For she said, 'If only I may touch His clothes, I shall be made well'. Immediately the fountain of her blood was dried up, and she felt in her body that she was healed of the affliction. And Jesus, immediately knowing in Himself that power had gone out of Him, turned around in the crowd and said, 'Who touched My clothes?' But His disciples said to Him, 'You see the multitude thronging You, and You say, "Who touched Me?"' And He looked around to see her who had done this thing. But the woman, fearing and trembling, knowing what had happened to her, came and fell down before Him and told Him the whole truth. And He said to her, 'Daughter, your faith has made you well. Go in peace, and be healed of your affliction.' While He was still speaking, some came from the ruler of the synagogue's house who said, 'Your daughter is dead. Why trouble the Teacher any further?' As soon as Jesus heard the word that was spoken, He said to the ruler of the synagogue, 'Do not be afraid; only believe'. And He permitted no one to follow Him except Peter, James, and John the brother of James. Then He came to the house of the ruler of the synagogue, and saw a tumult and those who wept and wailed loudly. When He came in, He said to them, 'Why make this commotion and weep? The child is not dead, but sleeping'. And they ridiculed Him. But when He had put them all outside, He took the father and the mother of the child, and those who were with Him, and entered where the child was lying. Then He took the child by the hand, and said to her, 'Talitha, cumi', which is translated, 'Little girl, I say to you, arise'. Immediately the girl arose and walked, for she was twelve years of age. And they were overcome with great amazement. But He commanded them strictly that no one should know it, and said that something should be given her to eat."

Mark 5 verses 21-43

"While He spoke these things to them, behold, a ruler came and worshiped Him, saying, 'My daughter has just died, but come and lay Your hand on her and she will live'. So Jesus arose and followed him, and so did His disciples. And suddenly, a woman who had a flow of blood for twelve years came from behind and touched the hem of His garment. For she said to herself, 'If only I may touch His garment, I shall be made well'. But Jesus turned around, and when He saw her He said, 'Be of good cheer, daughter; your faith has made you well'. And the woman was made well from that hour. When Jesus came into the ruler's house, and saw the flute players and the noisy crowd wailing, He said to them, 'Make room, for the girl is not dead, but sleeping'. And they ridiculed Him. But when the crowd was put outside, He went in and took her by the hand, and the girl arose. And the report of this went out into all that land."

Matthew 9 verses 18-26

This woman considered her medical condition so serious she

interrupted Jesus, the Great Physician, on His way to an emergency call. It was like this: the only daughter of a man called Jairus, a ruler of the Jewish synagogue, was dying and her father put in an emergency call for Jesus to come and prevent her death. He fell down at the feet of the Lord in great distress making the urgent appeal on behalf of his beloved daughter.

But this woman was determined to have healing for herself first when she had the opportunity. Considering she had her condition 12 years, the urgency of the "house call" from Jairus, and the large crowd present, she must have felt desperate to do what she did in "jumping the queue". But in spite of her surreptitious interruption she is commended by the Lord for her faith which He duly rewarded by making her immediately whole.

How she went about this is unusual. She may have heard of those in Luke chapter 6 verse 19 who had come from all Judaea, Jerusalem, the sea coasts of Tyre and Sidon and were healed by just touching Jesus in public. She may have thought there was some magical influence and diffusion of power from His person and around Him, suggests Trench in his book on the miracles[87] but I doubt this as it was the "Hem of His garment," the blue in His prayer shawl tassel, she focused on touching. However, she wished to steal a personal, secret encounter with Jesus – impossible! She soon was shocked to find herself the centre of attraction in the large crowd after Jesus called her back to Himself following upon her touch of faith. A public consultation after the cure!

The Lord Jesus, being in His ministry a Jewish Rabbi as well as a Physician, would wear the tallith, a square shaped coarse outer garment on top of His kittuna, a long inner garment.

At each corner of the tallith was a tassel, the tsitsith, which had four long white threads with one of hyacinth knotted together.[88] This was the "Hem of His garment" and contained the blue colour representing Heaven. Numbers 15 verse 40 says: *"That you may remember, and do all my commandments, and be holy unto your God"*. The Lord Jesus was the Heavenly Man who was holy and who observed all the commandments of His Father God. He needed no remembrance to do so. Yet He subjected Himself to be subservient to the Law of Moses. He was the only person who magnified the Law and made it honourable. He had the intrinsic right to wear the blue ribbon on the border of His garment.

This lady must have been of child-bearing age but weak through chronic blood loss from her illness. She would be pale in appearance from anaemia with very pale sclerae, koilonychia[89] of her nails, and poor hair texture. She would be weak and probably somewhat breathless on exercise. She would be nervous at the thought of what she was about to do and it would have taken all her energy to force her way through the crowd which was thronging the Lord.

Her blood loss was evidently local rather than general in origin. This can be deduced from the words "flux of blood" in Matthew and "staunched" in Luke as to the site of cure. Hobart in page 15 of *"The Medical Language of Luke"* says of the Greek word *'histanai'* translated 'staunched' in the KJV: "This is the only passage in the New Testament where this word is used in this sense. It is the usual word in the medical writers to denote the stoppage of bodily discharges and especially such as mentioned here". Hence she possibly had a gynaecological malady such as menorrhagia, metrorrhagia or epi-menorrhagia. This would mean she could probably be childless as she had it for twelve years. But what in turn was the cause of this? Was it hormonal or pathological?

She would be more liable than usual to inter-current infection due to her weakened condition. We can see from the Gospel records that disease was rampant in communities at that time in Israel[90] when *"The whole city"* was at the door of the house where Jesus was, requesting healing from Him - a whole city needing a Doctor!

Religiously she would be unable to attend the Synagogue. Personally and domestically her life would be problematic and difficult – see Leviticus 15 verses 19-33.

Her condition, according to Luke in Chapter 8 verse 43, was incurable. Mark in his Gospel (Chapter 5 verse 26) is critical of the Medical Profession of his day, saying that the Doctors had made her worse. Indeed, they had caused her more distress by leaving her destitute financially as well as not curing her. This is against the first law of Medicine, well known from the time of the Greek physicians: *"Primum non nocere"* i.e. do (the patient) no harm. It became included in the Hippocratic oath taken by Doctors on qualification as: "… abstain from doing harm".[91]

More pertinent to this case, John Lightfoot in his commentary on Mark 5 verse 26 quotes R. Jochanan: "Bring (or take) a gum of Alexandria the weight of a zuzee and of alum, the weight of a zuzee and of crocus hortensis the weight of a zuzee: let these be bruised together and be given in wine to the woman that hath an issue of blood. But if this does not benefit, take of Persian onions thrice three logs, boil them in wine and then give it to her to drink and say: 'Arise from thy flux'." He goes on: "If this does not prevail, set her in a place where two ways meet and let her hold a cup of wine in her hand and let someone come from behind her and affrighten her and say: 'Arise from thy flux'."

"But if that do no good, take a handful of cummin and a handful of crocus and a handful of foenum groenum. Let these be boiled in wine, and give them to her to drink and say: 'Arise from thy flux'."

Over ten other prescriptions are given, seeking a cure for the patient![92]

Luke would be conversant with such varied treatments, both orthodox for the time, and quackery, but in view of current attempts at treatment Mark would be justified in his comments regarding this poor woman's suffering of: *"Many things from many physicians. She had spent all that she had and was no better, but rather grew worse"*.

It was not until William Harvey, Physician to King James I and Charles I, published *'De Motu Cordis'* in 1628 that the function of the heart and the circulation of the blood were known.[93] Even after this, many doctors and quacks were hard to convince, and Harvey suffered rejection for the truth of his findings, even from his own profession.

What was in her mind in believing that to touch the border of blue would produce healing is uncertain. Perhaps there was an element of religious superstition. The other synoptic Gospels tell her obsession was such that *she kept saying: "If I could only touch His clothes"*. But, in the Gospel of Luke, Jesus asks who touched *Him*. Perhaps she appreciated something of the meaning of the blue in the tassel. She seemed, in spite of her imperfect faith, to have realised that it was not just what Jesus did but who He was! Power went out of Him and He knew that personal touch of faith, albeit imperfect, in a crowd that was thronging Him. Also, He knew it was a woman who touched Him, not a man (Mark 5 verse 32); the omniscience of Christ as well as the power of Christ.

It is said the word 'virtue' used in the translation of *'dynamis'* (power) in Luke 8 verse 46 is used in the old medical sense of the power of force which brings about a definite result.[94] People spoke of the soporific 'virtue' of this or that drug. The term is used in Luke 5 verse 17 and Mark 5 verse 30 with such technical precision for the supernatural power that it suggests that it flowed out at the touch of faith.

It may be noteworthy that in touching the "hem of His garment" she was touching the clothes of the one whose train filled the Temple in Isaiah 6. Isaiah saw the Son of God in Glory (John 12 verse 41): she sees Him in flesh. Isaiah could not touch Him in Glory: she touched Him in the streets of Galilee.

Her condition of 12 years was cured in a moment. This was no symptomatic treatment but a radical cure. Jesus, the Great Physician, cured her without stating a diagnosis! She felt well immediately - Luke 8 verse 47; Mark 5 verse 29 - and this bleeding would not return – Mark 5 verse 34 and Luke 8 verse 48. She was sent into peace in Luke`s account and into perfect health in Mark's account. She would feel as if she had had a blood transfusion! Also, the psychological lift and physical benefit of not needing protective clothing for her problem would be a great comfort. Moreover, she could now live normal life religiously, domestically and socially again.

Jesus would not let her steal away unnoticed however. He summoned her back to make a public confession to the crowd regarding the circumstances of her personal contact with Him. Imagine a Doctor making the patient tell all those in a full waiting room all her/his problems publicly! But this was not to embarrass her but to establish her faith in Him and let the people know how she was cured or 'saved'. It was her testimony to all.

However, she would now need to go home and do housework, such as bed washing and washing of her clothes (Leviticus 15 verse 26), and take a job, depending on circumstances. But she had the strength now. It may even be not too late to have children - or more children!

She was now cured physically but ceremonially she would bring her offering on the eighth day after her cleansing to the priest, two turtle doves or two young pigeons according to the Law of God. The one was for a sin offering and the other for a burnt offering to make atonement for herself (Leviticus 15 verses 28-33).

But, most importantly, she had entered into salvation. Saved by her faith in Jesus, not just as a Physician but as the Messiah of her nation who had become her personal Saviour and who now addressed her as: '*Daughter*' in spite of the inadequate or unorthodox approach to Him. She was sent away into peace and dignity. She had come to touch His clothes, now she had been touched at the depths of her being by the penetrating power of the Son of God. She had expected to be healed from the outside in. She found healing from the inside out. She was truly healed!

One wonders if such was the experience of those who are reported in Mark 6 verse 56 as touching the border of His clothes as He passed by in the street. They were all healed of their sickness but did they go into peace?

We are reminded in this miracle that healing had a cost for Jesus. He was not a magician. We see here the harmony in His nature of Deity and Humanity in the miracle. There was the infusion of Divine power from Him at her touch and yet "*Virtue went out of Him*" showing His humanity.

The woman's problem lay within herself, through no fault of her own. But she realised she needed outside help from another. She found that only Jesus could deal with her problem, having tried other remedies and people. She was "at the end of the line". So with sin - it is an internal and personal problem, present initially through no fault of our own. We inherit sin from Adam but we can find the remedy in Jesus Christ, the Last Adam, the Great Physician. We need not wait till we have tried all else first!

She needed power to live. The same power she obtained through a simple touch of faith is available to any who wish to touch Him in saving faith today. They will receive His power and be made whole. This is made good to us by His death on the cross. "*When we were yet without strength, in due time Christ died for the ungodly*" (Romans 5 verse 6).

[87]Trench Richard Chenevix, 11th edition revised Macmillan and Co. 1876, *"Notes on the Miracles of our Lord"*.

[88]Edersheim Alfred, *"The Life and Times of Jesus the Messiah"*, Vol.1, pages 622-624.

[89]Hollow shape of the nails sometimes called spooning.

[90]Mark 1 verse 33

[91]We know from the writings of Heroditus (5th Century BC) that cures were performed in the past such as enemas and blood-letting. He also advised diet and exercise with the application of oils in the prevention and treatment of disease. Hippocrates, who lived 460-370 BC, performed treatments such as cautery. Although the Ancients called the blood: the 'River of life', they performed venesection, cupping, and 'alternatives' for diseases. The former two would certainly make the patient worse! 'Alternatives' were varied herbs, some of which were haemostatic and applied to 'adjust the sanguine humour'. Some were applied directly to the source of bleeding! Galen of Pergamum, 129-216 BC, the most celebrated Doctor of the Roman Empire and Physician to the Emperor Marcus Aurelius, who also studied Medicine in Egypt, the most advanced University of that time, advised clinical observation and the value of the pulse in diagnosis. His thoughts pervaded Medicine till the Renaissance and beyond. Dioscardes, a Greek Physician in 1 AD, produced a Pharmacopoeia of medicinal plants and substances for varied uses. Celcus, 25 BC - 50 AD, had other remedies. In *'De Medicina'* book V, he advised for suppression of bleeding: blacking (chalcanthon) to the Greeks, copper ore, acacia, lycium with water, lign-aloe, gums, lead sulphide, leek, polygonium, Cimolian chalk or potter's clay, antimony sulphide, cold water, wine, vinegar, alum from melos, iron and copper scales, etc.! To agglutinate a wound: myrrh, frankincense, gums, a sponge squeezed out of cold water, wine or vinegar, unscoured wool squeezed out of the same..."

In addition, incantations, magic bones, etc. would be used by some, much like the witch doctors of Africa today.

[92]https://www.studylight.org/commentaries/jlc/mark-5.html

[93]Harvey first "showed that arteries and veins form a complete circuit. The circuit starts at the heart and leads back to the heart. The heart's regular contractions drive the flow of bloods around the whole body". This was the first major advance in understanding the function of the heart and circulatory system. For 400 years, Doctors had followed the teaching of Galen and blood-letting was widely practised as a treatment, obviously doing more harm to the patient in the vast majority of cases. This would especially be so in anyone who was already anaemic through loss of blood as this poor woman.

[94]Lockyer Herbert, *"All the Miracles of the Bible"*, Zondervan Grand Rapids Michigan, page 194

The Case of long-term sickness in the hospital at Jerusalem
(The man who had an infirmity 38 years)

"After this there was a feast of the Jews, and Jesus went up to Jerusalem. Now there is in Jerusalem by the Sheep Gate a pool, which is called in Hebrew, Bethesda, having five porches. In these lay a great multitude of sick people, blind, lame, paralyzed, waiting for the moving of the water. For an angel went down at a certain time into the pool and stirred up the water; then whoever stepped in first, after the stirring of the water, was made well of whatever disease he had. Now a certain man was there who had an infirmity thirty-eight years. When Jesus saw him lying there, and knew that he already had been in that condition a long time, He said to him, 'Do you want to be made well?' The sick man answered Him, 'Sir, I have no man to put me into the pool when the water is stirred up; but while I am coming, another steps down before me'. Jesus said to him, 'Rise, take up your bed and walk'. And immediately the man was made well, took up his bed, and walked. And that day was the Sabbath. The Jews therefore said to him who was cured, 'It is the Sabbath; it is not lawful for you to carry your bed'. He answered them, "He who made me well said to me, 'Take up your bed and walk.'" Then they asked him, 'Who is the Man who said to you, "Take up your bed and walk"?' But the one who was healed did not know who it was, for Jesus had withdrawn, a multitude being in that place. Afterward Jesus found him in the temple, and said to him, 'See, you have been made well. Sin no more, lest a worse thing come upon you'. The man departed and told the Jews that it was Jesus who had made him well."

John 5 verses 1-15

This hospital would have been situated on a lovely spot in the city of Jerusalem; an architect-designed building with a pool, having five porches for shade. The flavour of this struck me on a visit to the "Etablissement Thermaux" at Vichy, France, some years ago where under the high porticos, sick people sat or lay waiting to "Take the waters". But this is Bethesda meaning 'the House of Mercy', the Jerusalem hospital.

According to Byzantine tradition, it was very near the reputed home of Joachim and Anne, the parents of Mary the mother of Jesus and the place of her birth. The church of St Anne was built on this site.

It was, according to the Bible, near the Sheep Gate which was on the North East side of Jerusalem, the place where it is said the sheep came into the city for sacrifice at the Temple.

John in his Gospel records the date of this miracle; a feast of the Jews was near. There have been various suggestions as to what feast this was:

- The theologian F.W.Farrar considered it to be the Feast of Purim. However, the Feast of Purim was said to be celebrated in local synagogues not in Jerusalem at the Temple.
- Lightfoot and Neander propose the Feast of Passover.
- Calvin and Bengel the Feast of Pentecost.
- Others suggest the Feast of Tabernacles in the year 28 AD.
- Edersheim calls it the 'Unknown Feast' and suggests the 'Feast of Wood-gathering' or New Year`s Day in the beginning of Autumn.

Whichever feast it was, there would be a buzz about the city with an abundance of pilgrims and many sheep being driven through the gate for sacrifice as pilgrims brought their offerings.

Have you ever known a hospital not to be busy? This one was

no different. There were people crowding the medical ward, the eye ward, the orthopaedic ward, the long-term sick ward, all waiting for a special visit from someone for healing. Not a nurse nor a Doctor, but an angel! It was believed that at certain times an angel came to disturb the water of the pool and the first person into it after this was cured, no matter the type or stage of the illness.

Although some believe the reference to an angel is an interpolation of the text in these verses in John`s Gospel, in Revelation 9 verse 14 four angels are said to be in charge of the river Euphrates, and in chapter 16 verse 12 one angel dries up that mighty river. Also in verse 4 of the same chapter an angel turns "the rivers and fountain of waters" to blood!

Even the Roman god Pan was associated with water and there is an alcove in the rock cliff at the main source of the Jordan River at Banias (Caesarea Philippi of the Bible), where a statue of Pan was placed and worshipped.

It has also been suggested an underground spring bubbling up caused an intermittent disturbance of the pool which people attributed to an angel.

Excavations have revealed a conduit from an upper pool[95] through a rock tunnel may have been the cause as a sluice gate regulated the flow of water from the higher pool when water levels were high[96].

David Stern in his Jewish New Testament commentary quotes the 'Encyclopaedia Judaica' saying: "Excavations have revealed that a health rite took place there during the Roman period" [9:1539]. Those attending were devotees of the Roman god Serapis and Greek god Asclepius, the god of medicine[97].

To this hospital comes One greater than the angels and the gods of Greece and Rome and who can indeed cure all disease. One man recumbent in the waiting area, one lost sheep near the sheep gate causes Jesus to focus on him. His muscles were wasted and contracted due to thirty eight years of inactivity. A sorry sight, the Lord Jesus seeks to encourage hope. *"Do you want to be made whole?"* He asks him.

The man`s thinking and response is based on the traditional angelic story and replies that he has no helper to get him into the pool at the vital moment. He tries and tries to get into the pool himself but his own efforts are in vain as he is preceded to the water every time by the more mobile. What a pathetic picture of loneliness, inadequate self-help and frustration. Yet he keeps on trying in spite of the difficulty of the steep and slippery steps. How like human attempts at salvation! Trusting not trying is the key. "By *grace* are you saved, through faith and that not of yourselves, it is the *gift* of God, not of works…" (Ephesians 2 verses 8 & 9).

The Lord Jesus, having received tacit permission by the man to help him, immediately transforms his mindset, commands him to get up, take his pallet of a bed, (the bed of the poor), and walk. Amazingly, he believes the word and does what he is told. He has faith in Jesus` word. *"Faith comes by hearing, and hearing by the word of God"* declares Romans 10 verse 17. He has received immediate power and restoration without human assistance, after-care, physiotherapy or support.

This is how a person is "saved" spiritually. Paul says: *"When we were without strength, in due time Christ died for the ungodly"*. Christ takes the initial move and He waits on a response. He died, was buried and rose again to give us power to live and makes this good to us by His Spirit given to live in us as a gift when we believe in Him. *"You shall receive power when the Holy Spirit has come upon you"* (Acts 1 verse 8).

He could now walk normally. No limp, no evidence of past disease, a perfect salvation for his body. He could, of course, have some issues ahead with family or friends. Perhaps broken relationships needed mending. No-one appears to have been visiting him in the hospital very much, if at all! This was a long-term illness, life outside goes on. Relatives and family adjust their priorities and may not be there when the patient needs that extra help. Nursing attendance is not mentioned, Florence Nightingale was not yet born! He would have to look for work now as there would be items of personal responsibility. But he now had the power to work these issues out for himself. He would now be living life 'outside the institution'.

Opposition now arose. The people who could and did not help him now criticised him. He was carrying his bed on the Sabbath, thus breaking Sabbath rules according to their view (see verse 10). He was working! A man who was lame for 38 years now working! *'Deo gratias!'* No congratulations from the Jews present. Paul, in 2 Timothy 3 verse 5, says: *"Having a form of godliness but denying its power"*. David Stern says although the Mishna makes carrying in a public area on Shabbat unlawful, in a walled city like Jerusalem a special legal arrangement called an *'eruv'* made it legal. In his Commentary he gives various possibilities for the decision of the Jews[98]. No matter, they failed to see the glory of God in the miracle through their prejudice.

Jesus indeed was accused of Sabbath breaking as well, as it was He who had commanded the man to carry his bed and walk. The man did not know who Jesus was till he met Him in the Temple where he had gone to give special thanks to God[99] as Jewish custom enjoined. It seems the Lord sought him out now specifically to give further instruction and some admonition. He was warned to forsake the sin which had resulted in his condition. Whatever Jesus meant, the man would understand. The Lord kept it private but he was expected to live a God-honouring life from now on.

But whether in ignorance of the rising hostility to Jesus because of His miracles on the Sabbath, or amazing ingratitude by perhaps seeking to curry favour with the Jewish leaders, or seeking to bear testimony, he went to the critics of the Lord to inform on the identity of his Benefactor. He may even, in a strange way, have resented Jesus knowing and judging his past sin(s) even although he was now healed by Him. People have strange reactions at times, even to good! Whatever, this resulted in intensification of persecution against Jesus with death threats – see verse 16.

It was commendable that the man went to the Temple to thank God for his cure, but there was no need to identify the Lord to His enemies. Jesus had conveyed Himself away from the pool after the healing in anonymity as a crowd was now gathering. He did not seek publicity for His good works or place Himself in unnecessary danger.

In His controversy with the Jews, the Lord, however, showed them He was working *with* God, His Father, and not against Him in the context of Sabbath observance (verses 17-19). The Lord shows in His statement: *"My Father has been working up until now, and I have been working"* (verse 17) that Sabbath observance is not always negative. His Father God works good on the Sabbath and He indeed was shown what to do by His Father and as such had the right to heal this man on the Sabbath day.

But persecution exploded into violent threats when Jesus said God was *His own* Father. "His Father in a peculiar sense, making His action on same level as the action of God."[100]

The miracle in the hospital was healing for the man but increased the hostility of the Jews to Jesus. Bethesda, the House of Mercy, had now become the house of judgment and violence. The lame man was released from immobility and judgment but Jesus was judged wrongly for His good work. The wrong judgment later causing His death on a cross made our freedom possible when He was judged for us. *"He was delivered for our offences, and was raised again for our justification."*

The Lord Jesus later in John 7 verses 22 and 23 seeks to explain that the healing of the man on the Sabbath should have been acceptable to the Jews even on humanitarian grounds employing an *a priori* argument. Circumcision was performed on the Sabbath even if the eighth day, the time to be circumcised, fell on a Sabbath. Thus *total* healing of the body should surely take precedence over "ceremonial cleansing" of *part* of the body. It was, therefore, not a violation of the Law of Moses. Appeal was made by the Lord for just and considered judgment on the issue and a re-examination of their view about the Sabbath.

This man's illness was as a result of some sin bringing upon himself the moral judgment of God. Such must have been serious as he paid dearly in severity and duration, but Jesus has mercy upon him. Not all judgment is future. There is moral judgment now on earth. In Exodus 20, God says He visits the iniquity of the fathers upon the children to the third and fourth generations of those who hate Him but shows mercy to thousands of those who love Him and keep His commandments. What was the sin? The disciples never asked. Rightly so, Jesus would not have told them. He was a Physician.

It is good also for Christians to remember that judgment first begins at the house of God (1 Peter 4 verse 17). But if it first begins with the believers, what will the end be of those who obey not the gospel? - moral *and* penal judgment!

The question could be asked: Why did Jesus not heal *all* the sick at Bethesda Hospital? Why this man only? He had the power, He was Jehovah-Ropheca in flesh, the God who heals. Also, why did He not raise all the dead in John 11? Why just Lazarus? In the first case, answers heard have included: "The Sovereignty of God", Jesus "Chose the worst case scenario" and "This man represented Israel's failure of 40 years in the wilderness"[101] but He healed all that came to Him at Capernaum in His early ministry! (see Mark 1 verse 34).

It could be said that this man suffered long the government of God in his life just like the Nation of Israel in their refusal to enter the Land of Promise.

In every case of *healing* in John the Lord dealt with individuals but each was a sign of a deeper truth. His focus was to show that *"Jesus is the Christ, the Son of God; and that believing you may have life in His name"* (John 20 verse 31).

Also, this is His First Coming into the world, clothed in humanity and humility. Surely at this time it would not have fitted the Divine plan for such display of mass public healing in Jerusalem at the time of His rejection. *"The Son of Man must suffer many things, and be rejected by the elders and chief priests and scribes,and be killed, and be raised the third day"* (Luke 9 verse 22). His prime work was the work of Salvation not healing.

---

[95]2 Kings 18 verse 17

[96]"Yesterday" Channel documentary "Forbidden History" with Jamie Theakston and Dr Shimon Gibson in Jerusalem on 19th June 2018.

[97]Oxford Archaeological Guides: *"The Holy Land"*, Oxford University Press, pages 28-31.

[98]Stern David H, *"Jewish New Testament Commentary"*, Jewish New Testament Publications, page 169

[99]Edersheim Alfred, *"Sketches of Jewish Social Life"*, page 153.

[100]Westcott`s *"St. John"*, James Clark and Co. Ltd. London 1958 edition, page 84.

[101]Tom Rice, Society for the Distribution of Hebrew Scriptures, points out every healing miracle in John`s Gospel reflects something of Israel`s history.

The Ear, Nose and Throat Case
(The deaf and dumb man)

"Again, departing from the region of Tyre and Sidon, He came through the midst of the region of Decapolis to the Sea of Galilee. Then they brought to Him one who was deaf and had an impediment in his speech, and they begged Him to put His hand on him. And He took him aside from the multitude, and put His fingers in his ears, and He spat and touched his tongue. Then, looking up to heaven, He sighed, and said to him, 'Ephphatha', that is, 'Be opened'. Immediately his ears were opened, and the impediment of his tongue was loosed, and he spoke plainly. Then He commanded them that they should tell no one; but the more He commanded them, the more widely they proclaimed it. And they were astonished beyond measure, saying, 'He has done all things well. He makes both the deaf to hear and the mute to speak.'"

Mark 7 verses 31-37

This case which interested Mark so much was probably narrated to him by the Apostle Peter, an eye witness. Although the problem of speech and hearing are not life-threatening, they are very personal and socially incapacitating. The miracle is told in detail and I have classified it as an ENT case. Matthew only mentions "the dumb" among other class lists of diseases being healed.[102] Mark who in his Gospel portrays Jesus as The Perfect Servant of Jehovah emphasises the fulfilment of Isaiah's prophecy: *"Then ... the ears of the deaf shall be unstopped ... and the tongue of the dumb sing"*.[103]

Although Jesus never in His ministry is recorded as leaving Israel,

He visits the region of Decapolis, the Roman heathen cities in Israel mainly on the East of the Jordan.[104] These cities were independent and subject only to the Governor of Syria but were in close contact with the Jews of that area as Matthew 15 verse 31 shows when they *"glorified the God of Israel"* after Jesus, the Jewish Rabbi and Physician, healed so many on a mountainside in their territory.

The Lord is presented now with the case of a man who is deaf and has an impediment in his speech. Isaiah says of Messiah, speaking to the Gentiles, *"Bring out ... the deaf who have ears ... that you may know and believe Me, and understand that I am He. Before Me there was no God formed, nor shall there be after Me"*;[105] a very relevant application of this prophecy to this particular case in this particular society with Roman gods.

This patient, a Gentile, has difficulty in comprehension and communication. He has been brought to Jesus by his friends. (Three individuals are brought to Jesus in the Gospels: In Mark 2 a paralysed man is brought; in Mark 8 a blind man is brought. Now, this deaf and dumb man is brought.)

Deaf and dumb people are very self-conscious with a feeling of isolation. He may well have needed encouragement to come. So did many of us in coming to Jesus, but the Holy Spirit was the Person who brought us to the Saviour.

The speech problem would be secondary to his hearing problem. He would most likely have become deaf when he was developing speech in infancy. In a survey done in 2006-7, 57% of deafness was due to unknown causes. This could also have developed from genetic syndromes (over 60%), anti-natal insult of varying causes, childhood infection such as meningitis, glue ear, other varied diseases of the ear and trauma to the head.

He was unable to articulate proper speech, soft sounds

being particularly difficult. Sound perception would lead to a communication problem, social isolation, insecurity, failure to achieve in life and perhaps even suffer bullying, especially when young. Hearing is so important in life. The Lord Jesus would say: "*He who has ears to hear, let him hear*" in a spiritual context to the people in the Gospels but: "*He who has an ear, let him hear*" He says repeatedly in the book of Revelation chapters 2 and 3 to the churches. The churches are more deaf now!

With so many voices in the world, people are confused who or what to believe. The Lord Jesus says: "Take heed *what* you hear".[106] Who do we listen to? What do we listen to? He also says: "Take heed *how* you hear".[107] What is our response to what we hear? In both, the context in the Bible is future revelation. There is nothing hidden that will not be revealed! This would apply today not only to the ear gate but also to the eye gate – especially social media, TV, books, magazines, etc. but also who or what we look at in every day life.

The man's friends had their own idea as to how Jesus would heal him. They besought Him, "*they begged Him to put His hand on him*" (verse 32). How typical of our thoughts concerning the way God should work, even *when* He should work; our ideas instead of God`s. But of the Servant Physician, Isaiah says: "*Hear, you deaf; … who is blind … as the Lord`s servant … opening the ears, but He does not hear*".[108] He needs not our advice and does not need to follow our plans.

Jesus takes him aside from the crowd where there would be background noise and distraction and gives him personal attention, much as a Doctor takes a patient into the quietness of his/her surgery away from other people. The treatment was specific to this individual. God is a personal God and we are so individual in constitution. It is amazing how the one God who made us in His image is a God of infinite variety. Our faces are different, our eyes, our finger prints, our voices, our DNA is unique, our personalities are so distinct. We thus need individual attention from a personal Creator and Father. That is one of the reasons we pray. "Casting all your care upon Him, for He cares for *you*" (1 Peter 5 verse 7).

The Lord indicates through signs how He will heal him. The Perfect Servant first puts His fingers into his ears and thus blocks any residual hearing he may have and the external noise. This action focuses attention on the primary site of the problem. Picture the scene - Jesus is opposite this man, face to face, making him concentrate solely on Him. Professor Barclay says: "He acts out before the man what He is about to do".[109] He may not hear but he could see and feel touch. The Lord encourages his expectation. He puts His fingers in his ears. He gives of Himself in the saliva,[110] touches his tongue; tactile stimulus to the part about to be released. He looks to Heaven as a prayer to the Father who sent Him, thus showing the man, who is probably heathen, the source of all blessing and then sighs, thus showing His personal sympathy and commitment to him. He communicates with him in a way he could understand. He speaks to him not in Greek but in a chosen onomatopoeic word of His own language Aramaic, *Ephphatha*, a word that he could lip read – "*Be opened*". He responded immediately in faith and was cured of his affliction. The opening of the ears are mentioned first, then the tongue is freed. His hearing is perfect; his speech is now clear. The Master can cleanse a person's speech if they will open their ears to Him and believe His word. "*We ... believe and therefore speak*" (2 Corinthians 4 verse 13).

We often focus on the great global and national changes and events of the coming Kingdom of God, but one of the remarkable features is a pure speech. "*Then I will restore to the peoples a pure language ('Then I will purify the lips of the peoples' – NIV) that they all may call on the name of the Lord*" (Zephaniah 3 verse 9). "*Speak each man the truth to his neighbour ...*" (Zechariah 8 verse 16), a personal transformed feature of the tongue in the coming Kingdom. Imagine no swearing, no lies, no deceit, no exaggerations, no innuendo, but truth and blessing! Again we see here the Lord Jesus demonstrating the power of the age to come in His ministry.

In a live programme on TV in November 2016[111] a group of people were watched for their reaction when sound was switched on after a cochlear implant operation. Some patients could previously hear and had become deaf; one was born deaf. The report after the operation was that their speech was: "Like Mickey Mouse", high-pitched and rapid. Also: "rather tinny and hollow" to one person operated on who was giving testimony on the programme. The audiologist reassured them that the brain would interpret it more normally as time elapsed. Not so here, the speech was immediately perfect. No speech therapist was required for improvement. No follow up needed.

Mark keeps the original Aramaic language in his Gospel at noteworthy times:

- *Talitha, cumi* in Chapter 5 verse 41 when the young girl is being raised from the dead - such tenderness from the Master at such an emotional and sensitive time.
- *Abba* used by the Lord in prayer to His Father in the Garden of Gethsemane in Chapter 14 verse 36, the word of the child in the home to his father - such closeness and deep pathos.
- *Eloi, Eloi, lama sabachthani?* to His God on the Cross in Chapter 15 verse 34 after 3 hours of cosmic darkness. "God abandoned by God, who can understand that?" said Luther. The scapegoat of Leviticus 16 abandoned alone to the wilderness in Divine judgement.

The people were *"astonished beyond measure"* at the miracle - a flash reaction! God can change our lives in a moment of personal encounter with Jesus, the Great Physician, when we submit to His personal care and power. A reference to any Anatomy, Physiology,

Neurophysiology, Speech and Language or Psychology textbook with reference to hearing and speaking will show how amazing this miracle is in the light of current knowledge. The people who would be mainly Gentile only saw the visual effect of the miracle but glorified the God of Israel who was reaching out to them in their need.[112] Isaiah says: *"In Him shall the Gentiles trust"*. So it is today. *"Salvation is from the Jews."* Jesus was a Jew.

The Physician`s words are not followed however! Instead of the lack of publicity He requested, the people broadcast the healing. This was in spite of repeated emphatic instructions to the contrary. The Lord would have a reason for this prohibition. In the case of the cleansing of the leper, failure to obey this command led to the restriction of His movements and to a possible misunderstanding that He was working out-with the parameters of the Law of Moses. Perhaps also He was wishing to prioritise the preaching of the gospel rather than be known as a miracle-worker. Also, the West side of the Lake of Galilee was said to be a ferment of revolution at times. Lockyer suggests there was still the danger of the people wishing to make Him king - their kind of king - remembering the events of John 6.[113]

The people seem to recognise the two parts of the man's problem and declared: "He has done *all* things well". The Lord had dealt with both the hearing loss and the speech problem completely at one time and in an excellent manner. This was God's own verdict on His work in creation: *"God saw everything that He had made, and indeed it was very good"*.[114]

Messiah Himself had His ear opened and His tongue instructed: *"The Lord God has given Me the tongue of the learned, that I should know how to speak a word in season to him who is weary. He awakens Me morning by morning, He awakens My ear to hear as the learned. The Lord God has opened My ear; and I was not rebellious, nor did I turn away"*. The Lord's Servant, the Lord Jesus, opens this man's ears because His were opened and He heard instructions from His Father first! If we wish to serve Him well, we must do the same!

---

[102]Matthew 15 verse 30

[103]Isaiah 35 verses 5 & 6

[104]Page 40, note 83

[105]Isaiah 43 verses 8 & 10

[106]Mark 4 verse 24

[107]Luke 8 verse 18

[108]Isaiah 42 verse 18

[109]Barclay W: *"The Gospel of Mark"*, page 206

[110]The use of saliva (spit) in healing was only used by Jesus in two miracles, this one and the blind man of Bethsaida. Both were probably Gentiles and the use of saliva would assist faith. It was believed by Jew and Gentile to assist healing - not to be recommended today!

[111]"Breaking the Silence" - Channel 4 - November 2016

[112]Matthew 15 verse 31

[113]Lockyer Herbert: *"All the Miracles of the Bible"*, Zondervan, page 209

[114]Genesis 1 verse 31

The two stage Operation
(The blind man of Bethsaida)

"Then He came to Bethsaida; and they brought a blind man to Him, and begged Him to touch him. So He took the blind man by the hand and led him out of the town. And when He had spit on his eyes and put His hands on him, He asked him if he saw anything. And he looked up and said, 'I see men like trees, walking'. Then He put His hands on his eyes again and made him look up. And he was restored and saw everyone clearly. Then He sent him away to his house, saying, 'Neither go into the town, nor tell anyone in the town'."

Mark 8 verses 22-26

This miracle is unique. It is the only one that Jesus, the Great Physician, did in two stages. All the other miracles were instantaneous in effect, even the deaf man with the impediment in his speech which involved two organs of the body. Why was this one different? Let us look at the record of Mark.

The man had friends who were interested in him. They did not leave him to beg like others although he was blind. They sought help for him when the opportunity sprang up with the coming of Jesus into town.

Again, they had their own ideas as to how the Lord should work. A touch would do. At least they had faith in the Rabbi from the other side of the lake. This healing is performed in Bethsaida Julias,[115] on the North East side of the Lake of Galilee, the city so named after Julia the infamous daughter of the Emperor Augustus.

Jesus takes a firm grip of the blind man's hand and leads him out of town. Why out of town? To give Himself peace to work, as there was a large crowd present, and to afford privacy for His patient. But also, this city was already becoming a place of unbelief, so the Lord removed him from the city and its culture. He spent precious time with the man and encouraged his faith using tactile stimuli; spitting in his eyes and putting His hands on him. It is only on the East side of the Lake that Jesus is reported as using saliva directly for a cure. (In John 9 verse 6, He makes an ointment of clay with His saliva.) The other person was the deaf and dumb man from one of the Decapolis, Gentile cities, who was also taken aside from the crowd. Faith in the Lord Jesus here required assistance on the human side.

"Spittle was highly esteemed by the Jews in this respect, but here its efficacy is connected with the person of Him who used it" said J.N. Darby. "'Saliva jejuna' was reckoned as a remedy for blindness" said Pliny. "Christ was clothing the supernatural in the form of the natural" says Lockyer. This was the spit of healing. Contrast the thought with the hatred of men using vile spit when Jesus was before the High Priest or the spit of contempt from the Roman soldiers toward the Lord at His trials.

Jesus questions him on his progress of recovery. The blind man sees men as trees walking. He distinguishes indistinct shapes and movement. He knew what trees and people looked like, so he was not born blind. The problem lay within himself not the trees or men. He is now making progress but his perception of reality is blurred. He did not need to go to "Specsavers," the Saviour was still here! How often is a person's appreciation of the reality of Christ blurred! This is especially so in the meaning of His death. Let the truth of His Word, the Bible, penetrate into our hearts.

Further attention is focused on him with Jesus putting His hands on his eyes again and making him look up, the source of all blessing coming from above. This is not magic but miracle. Having looked up, he begins to see clearly.

Remark has been made on the different words used for sight in the original Greek in verses 23 and 24 in "St Mark - *The Cambridge Greek Testament for Schools and Colleges*".[116] In verse 23, the Lord asked the man if he 'saw' anything. The man replies in verse 24. The Revised Version translates this next verse as: "*I see men, for I behold them as trees walking*". In verses 23 and 24, the word used first *'blepo'* means 'mental vision or consideration'. The second one *'orao'* applies to bodily sight. We ourselves as believers see Jesus now with the eye of faith, later with the eye of a glorified body.

But the progression of recovery in sight is note-worthy in the use of the word *'dieblepsen'* translated "looked steadily" in the Greek text of Sir A. F. Hort[117] and "looked steasfastly" by the "*Cambridge Greek Testament for Schools and Colleges*" as an instantaneous act of sight and then after restoration he began and continued to see all things clearly - *'eneblepsen'*, the imperfect tense of *'emblepo'*.

This shows the detailed skilful working of the Lord being described as by a Medical Student witnessing an operation being performed by a Consultant Surgeon. But here there is immediate recovery without eye drops, eye patch, bandaging and follow up appointments. Did Peter as a witness describe this event in such specific detail to Mark?

One can see in this miracle a picture of a backslider. The word used in verse 25 *'apokatestathe'* - restored - would suggest this. Also, the man knew what trees and men looked like. The word means: "a perfect restoration to the original state". As such he needed the second touch of the Saviour for full restoration.

The effort of the Lord Jesus in the work of restoration is worthy of note. One has said: "The sheep that was lost in Luke 15, a picture of a sinner, was certainly found by the Shepherd. The one in Matthew 18, a picture of the backslider, has the statement, '*If so be* that he find it'. Here there is doubt. The Shepherd seems to have had a greater search for the latter. Perhaps this sheep did not want to be found!" [118]

The context of the miracle reflects on the blindness of the disciples who have seen two great miracles in the feeding of the 5,000 and 4,000 yet are spiritually blind as to their significance as verse 21 shows. It is noteworthy that the miracle of the feeding of the 5,000 registered well with that multitude since they wished to make Jesus their king at once - by force! *"The children of this world are in their generation wiser than the children of light."* [119] The disciples themselves were in need of a second touch. So often we do too, and a third and fourth!

Why is this man sent quietly home and forbidden to talk about his sensational cure? I think it is because his faith being weak, the people of the city would be of no help in the progress of *spiritual* recovery. Let him consider this event at home and be *"rooted and built up in Him, and established in the faith."* [120] After all, the city of Bethsaida, although the city of Peter, Andrew and Philip, was later pronounced with "Woe" from the Lord because of its lack of faith - as were other surrounding towns which had witnessed so many of His mighty works. The Lord removed the blind man from this area of unbelief to minister to him, so why send him back to such a situation at this early time in his recovery?

It is interesting that the Lord in this itinerary tells the man, earlier healed, who was deaf and dumb and his friends, the blind man and his friends here, and the three disciples who were on the Mount of Transfiguration not to tell others. It is seldom wise to ask new converts or restored backsliders to immediately testify publicly unless convinced of the Lord`s command, or for disciples to broadcast supernatural experiences of Christ.

[115]Some scholars, as Young in his Concordance at page 92 and F. W. Farrar, *"The Life of Christ"* at page 189, think that there were two places called Bethsaida; others such as A. F. Hort say that the 'Other side' in Mark 8 is the other side of the bay at the North of the Lake of Galilee and that there is only one Bethsaida (see his *"The Gospel according to Mark"*, page 106, note 45 and page 118 note 22). I take the latter view that there is only one Bethsaida in Scripture.

[116]*"St Mark - Cambridge Greek Testament for Schools and Colleges"*, 1889, page 117

[117]"St Mark", Cambridge University Press 1914, page 118

[118]Jack Hunter, Kilmarnock (paraphrased)

[119]Luke 16 verse 8

[120]Colossians 2 verse 7

The Congenital Disease Case
(The man born blind)

*"Now as Jesus passed by, He saw a man who was blind from birth.
And His disciples asked Him, saying, 'Rabbi, who sinned, this man
or his parents, that he was born blind?' Jesus answered, 'Neither
this man nor his parents sinned, but that the works of God should
be revealed in him. I must work the works of Him who sent Me
while it is day; the night is coming when no one can work. As long
as I am in the world, I am the light of the world.' When He had said
these things, He spat on the ground and made clay with the saliva;
and He anointed the eyes of the blind man with the clay. And He
said to him, 'Go, wash in the pool of Siloam' (which is translated,
Sent). So he went and washed, and came back seeing. Therefore
the neighbours and those who previously had seen that he was blind
said, 'Is not this he who sat and begged?' Some said, 'This is he'.
Others said, 'He is like him'. He said, 'I am he'. Therefore they
said to him, 'How were your eyes opened?' He answered and said,
'A Man called Jesus made clay and anointed my eyes and said to
me, "Go to the pool of Siloam and wash". So I went and washed,
and I received sight'. Then they said to him, 'Where is He?' He
said, 'I do not know'. They brought him who formerly was blind
to the Pharisees. Now it was a Sabbath when Jesus made the clay
and opened his eyes. Then the Pharisees also asked him again how
he had received his sight. He said to them, 'He put clay on my
eyes, and I washed, and I see'. Therefore some of the Pharisees said,
'This Man is not from God, because He does not keep the Sabbath'.
Others said, 'How can a man who is a sinner do such signs?' And
there was a division among them. They said to the blind man again,*

'What do you say about Him because He opened your eyes?' He said, 'He is a prophet'. But the Jews did not believe concerning him, that he had been blind and received his sight, until they called the parents of him who had received his sight. And they asked them, saying, 'Is this your son, who you say was born blind? How then does he now see?' His parents answered them and said, 'We know that this is our son, and that he was born blind; but by what means he now sees we do not know, or who opened his eyes we do not know. He is of age; ask him. He will speak for himself.' His parents said these things because they feared the Jews, for the Jews had agreed already that if anyone confessed that He was Christ, he would be put out of the synagogue. Therefore his parents said, 'He is of age; ask him'. So they again called the man who was blind, and said to him, 'Give God the glory! We know that this Man is a sinner.' He answered and said, 'Whether He is a sinner or not I do not know. One thing I know: that though I was blind, now I see.' Then they said to him again, 'What did He do to you? How did He open your eyes?' He answered them, 'I told you already, and you did not listen. Why do you want to hear it again? Do you also want to become His disciples?' Then they reviled him and said, 'You are His disciple, but we are Moses' disciples. We know that God spoke to Moses; as for this fellow, we do not know where He is from.' The man answered and said to them, 'Why, this is a marvellous thing, that you do not know where He is from; yet He has opened my eyes! Now we know that God does not hear sinners; but if anyone is a worshipper of God and does His will, He hears him. Since the world began it has been unheard of that anyone opened the eyes of one who was born blind. If this Man were not from God, He could do nothing.' They answered and said to him, 'You were completely born in sins, and are you teaching us?' And they cast him out. Jesus heard that they had cast him out; and when He had found him, He said to him, 'Do you believe in the Son of God?' He answered and said, 'Who is He, Lord, that I may believe in Him?' And Jesus said to him, 'You have both seen Him and it is He who is talking with you'. Then he said, 'Lord, I believe!' And he worshipped Him.

> *And Jesus said, 'For judgment I have come into this world, that those who do not see may see, and that those who see may be made blind'. Then some of the Pharisees who were with Him heard these words, and said to Him, 'Are we blind also?' Jesus said to them, 'If you were blind, you would have no sin; but now you say, "We see". Therefore your sin remains."*

John 9

This miracle of the Lord Jesus is powerfully significant in that as the blind man himself says in verse 32, *"Since the world began it has been unheard of that anyone opened the eyes of one who was born blind"*. Prophets had done miracles before but such a miracle was reserved for Messiah. Isaiah specifies concerning His ministry in chapter 35 verse 5: *"Then* shall the eyes of the blind be opened ..." and in chapter 42 verse 7 when listing some of the acts of the coming Servant of Jehovah, includes that He would *"Open blind eyes..."* - something not done before.

The man in the report was born blind. The question in the mind of the disciples was: "Why?" This is a question often asked by people: Why does a God of love allow suffering - especially in children? Why do the innocent suffer? Sometimes we just have to live without answers in this life.

We know that 'The Fall' in Eden allowed sin into the world and subsequently the reign of sin and death was established till the death and resurrection of Christ broke its power. However, the question asked specifically here was: *"Who* sinned, this man or his parents, that he was born blind?" Was it prenatal sin committed by the unborn child (a belief of some at this time), or was it moral judgment resulting from the sin of the parents (Exodus 20 verse 5).

The answer of the Lord was clear, *"Neither this man nor his parents sinned, but that the works of God should be revealed in him"*. Messiah was here in presence with power to deal with such a case as this.

However, the reply of Jesus showed that He knew the moral, spiritual and medical history of the man and both his parents – immediately! Also, He knew the purpose of God concerning him! He knows *our* genealogy and His purpose for our lives also. Did you or have you found it?

Verse 4 would indicate the Lord`s time was now short on earth and His work was now urgent. He is the Light of the world while here in the world. For sight we need light. The light must come from outside ourselves, for sight we need eyes to see in that light.

Jesus spits on the ground and makes clay, then anoints the eyes of the blind man with the clay. The spit was from within, the clay was from without, the man`s eyes were opened by the Light of the World.

Jesus spat on the ground, hence came down to earth`s level. Do we see a picture of the creation of man here or His Incarnation, or both? At any rate, the treatment has been given, now for the cure. The blind man was told to go and wash in the pool of Siloam which means 'sent'. 'Sent' is a key word in the writings of John. Jesus was always conscious of His Heavenly origin and earthly purpose; that He was the Sent One from God.

The word in Hebrew for pool is *'Berekah'*, used in Psalm 84 verse 6 of blessing. *"As they pass through the Valley of Baca, they make it a spring; the rain also covers it with pools."* He was sent for blessing.

Isaiah was sent to meet King Ahaz here with his son Shear-Jashub,[121] whose name means "a remnant shall return". A remnant of Israel shall see!

Rabshakeh stood here by the conduit of the upper pool to threaten Jerusalem 30 years later.[122]

The word 'Upper' is rendered "Most High" over thirty times

in Scripture, for example, the blessing of the Most High in Genesis 14 verse 18.[123] The conduit may have been Hezekiah's Tunnel, a channel of blessing. The 'end' of the blessing was in the Pool of Siloam to which the man was sent.

The man simply did what he was told, being probably led down to the pool as he was blind. By his obedience of faith he came into the blessing of the Most High God. He emerges from the pool, walks up the steps into the sunlight. No need for adjustment or protective sunglasses, he could now see for the first time in his life.

It seems that the man looked different now as there was a dispute as to his identity in verses 8 and 9. A person after being born again incurs an immediate change. They have received the Holy Spirit and become partakers of the Divine nature and this may lighten their appearance, especially the eyes.

He now gives an honest testimony as to what happened to him. Some things he knows, some things he does not know, verses 11 and 12. One thing he does know is who Jesus is, what Jesus did and what He said to him. The famous words since quoted by John Newton in his hymn 'Amazing Grace': "Once I was blind, now I can see."

The neighbours brought him to the Pharisees to be questioned a second time. The fact that it was the Sabbath on which the man had been given his sight was bad news to the religious experts. Jesus could not possibly be a Man of God to do this on the Sabbath!

He had broken 3 of their rules in this miracle: He used clay c.f. Mishna Shabbat 7:2; 24:3, He performed kneading by mixing the spit with clay and He was working on the Sabbath.

There is a division among the Pharisees and Jews concerning the orthodoxy and integrity of the Lord (verse 16) with further questioning of the man and his parents. He initially confesses Jesus to be a prophet (verse 17) but finally as spiritual light increases in his spirit, as the Son of God. The Lord finding him in the synagogue has brought him into the fullness of light and he worships Him (verse 38). Saving faith is gradual here.

The man meanwhile is excommunicated from the synagogue with all its privileges - religiously and socially. Such procedure was by three degrees according to David Stern:[124]

1 Rebuke - this lasted 7 days
2 Rejection - this lasted 30 days and needed 3 people for invocation. People had to stay 6 feet from him.
3 "Treated as dead."

(This would shed light on Luke 14 verses 26-33 about hating father and mother etc., to become a disciple.)

"Give glory to God", the instruction in verse 24 may mean: "Give glory to God, not this man who made you see because we know he is a sinner" or: "Swear to God you will tell the truth!" That is, the taking of an oath. That is: "We know this man is a sinner, swear we are telling the truth!"[125]

The Jews say to the man in verse 34: *"You were completely born in sins, and you are teaching us?"* The Hebrew word *'Mamzer'* used in verse 34 means: 'an illegitimate son'. (A son of a marriage prohibited by Law in Leviticus 18.) One who could not marry a legitimate daughter of Israel. They are slandering the man and therefore excluding him from any future marriage possibility under the law. He has met his first opposition in following Jesus! Yet as a new-born babe in Christ he immediately knew more spiritually than the so-called religious experts did!

This man may have had unprecedented healing but suffered

exclusion from the privileges of his Nation and the resources of his local synagogue/church. I reckon he would prefer his sight and the personal knowledge of the Son of God. No comparison!

---

[121]Isaiah 7 verse 3
[122]Isaiah 36 verse 2
[123]Jennings F.C. *"Studies in Isaiah"*, Loizeaux Brothers Neptune, New Jersey for a more complete explanation of the significance of the Hebrew words.
[124]*"Jewish New Testament Commentary"*, David H. Stern, Jewish New Testament Publications Inc., page 184
[125]Joshua 7 verse 19 and 1 Samuel 6 verse 5

The Multiple Syndrome Case
(The boy with epilepsy)

"And when they had come to the multitude, a man came to Him, kneeling down to Him and saying, 'Lord, have mercy on my son, for he is an epileptic and suffers severely; for he often falls into the fire and often into the water. So I brought him to Your disciples, but they could not cure him.' Then Jesus answered and said, 'O faithless and perverse generation, how long shall I be with you? How long shall I bear with you? Bring him here to Me.' And Jesus rebuked the demon, and it came out of him; and the child was cured from that very hour. Then the disciples came to Jesus privately and said, 'Why could we not cast it out?' So Jesus said to them, 'Because of your unbelief; for assuredly, I say to you, if you have faith as a mustard seed, you will say to this mountain, "Move from here to there", and it will move; and nothing will be impossible for you. However, this kind does not go out except by prayer and fasting.'"

Matthew 17 verses 14-21

And when He came to the disciples, He saw a great multitude around them, and scribes disputing with them. Immediately, when they saw Him, all the people were greatly amazed, and running to Him, greeted Him. And He asked the scribes, "What are you discussing with them?" Then one of the crowd answered and said, "Teacher, I brought You my son, who has a mute spirit. And wherever it seizes him, it throws him down; he foams at the mouth, gnashes his teeth, and becomes rigid. So I spoke to Your disciples that they should cast it out, but they could not." He answered him and said, "O faithless generation, how long shall I be with you? How long shall I bear with you? Bring him to Me." Then they brought him to Him. And when he saw Him, immediately the spirit convulsed him, and he fell on the ground and wallowed, foaming at the mouth. So He asked his father, "How long has this been happening to him?" And he said, "From childhood. And often he has thrown him both into the fire and into the water to destroy him. But if You can do anything, have compassion on us and help us." Jesus said to him, "If you can believe, all things are possible to him who believes." Immediately the father of the child cried out and said with tears, "Lord, I believe; help my unbelief!" When Jesus saw that the people came running together, He rebuked the unclean spirit, saying to it: "Deaf and dumb spirit, I command you, come out of him and enter him no more!" Then the spirit cried out, convulsed him greatly, and came out of him. And he became as one dead, so that many said, "He is dead." But Jesus took him by the hand and lifted him up, and he arose. And when He had come into the house, His disciples asked Him privately, "Why could we not cast it out?" So He said to them, "This kind can come out by nothing but prayer and fasting."

Mark 9 verses 14-29

"Now it happened on the next day, when they had come down from the mountain, that a great multitude met Him. Suddenly a man from the multitude cried out, saying, 'Teacher, I implore You, look on my son, for he is my only child. And behold, a spirit seizes him, and he suddenly cries out; it convulses him so that he foams at the mouth; and it departs from him with great difficulty, bruising him. So I implored Your disciples to cast it out, but they could not.' Then Jesus answered and said, 'O faithless and perverse generation, how long shall I be with you and bear with you? Bring your son here.' And as he was still coming, the demon threw him down and convulsed him. Then Jesus rebuked the unclean spirit, healed the child, and gave him back to his father."

Luke 9 verses 37-42

What is the diagnosis here? Did the boy have epilepsy? Was he demon-possessed or lunatic? The New King James Version of Matthew 17 verse 15 says he was an epileptic with a footnote "literally moonstruck". The Authorised Version says he was lunatic. The father in Mark 9 says his son had a dumb spirit and Luke says in chapter 9: "*A spirit takes him....*" Professor Swete on page 195 of his commentary on Mark says he was a demoniac. Is it possible that he had epilepsy, demon possession *and* a psychiatric problem which was affected by the moon? Ask any experienced hospital Accident and Emergency nurse and they will relate stories of the bizarre at the time of a full moon! Psalm 121 verse 6 says: "*The sun shall not strike you by day, nor the moon by night*". This is the promise of God in this Psalm of Ascents, sung by the pilgrims going up to the Feasts of the Lord at Jerusalem; very relevant with the full moon at the time of Passover as they camped by night in the valleys of Israel.

The boy had symptoms of epilepsy as seen in the description of the various stages of a fit: tonic, clonic and a stage of relaxation but he was clearly also demon-possessed. The Lord Jesus, the Great Physician, identified a spirit which produced deafness and dumbness and which was also described as unclean. Matthew clearly distinguishes lunacy from demon possession in Chapter 4 verse 24 in his list of miracles performed by the Lord Jesus: "*They brought to Him ... those who were demon-possessed, epileptics, and paralytics, and He healed them*".

It is noteworthy that Mark gives a fuller account of the miracle than Luke the Physician. Peter would have been an eyewitness, having come down from the Mount of Transfiguration with Jesus and James and John. He must have been so deeply impressed as his 'son' Mark, receiving this information from him, describes the miracle in such fine detail. Luke, seeing the social and domestic side of the problem, does however tell us that this boy was the only begotten son of his father.

The previous day in the Holy Mount there was the declaration concerning Jesus, the only begotten Son of *His* Father: *"This is My Beloved Son. Hear Him!"* But in the valley no one could hear this son, the beloved of *his* father – he was dumb. One Son seen in glory, the other in distress; the Father in the mount delighted, the father in the valley in despair. But the Son who was transfigured in glory came down to transform the son in distress!

Luke also tells us at the end of his account in verse 43 that they were all astonished at the *"mighty power of God"* (KJV), literally in the Greek text and so translated in the NKJV, "The majesty of God". Peter reflecting in his Second Epistle in Chapter 1 verse 16 tells us that when he was on the Mount of Transfiguration, the Holy Mount, they were *"eyewitnesses of His majesty"*. So we see the regal splendour of Divine power in both the mount *and* the valley. Thus the glory of His humanity is no less than the glory of His deity. *"In Him dwells all the fullness of the Godhead bodily."*[126]

The emotional distress of the father and the failure of the disciples at the foot of the mountain capture our attention. The crowd are witnesses to the argument between the disciples and the scribes. At least the disciples tried to help the man. But, in their own strength: "Why could not *we* cast it out?" (Mark 9 verse 28); prayer and self-denial were lacking. Worse, they dashed the father`s hope in the ability of the Lord Jesus to heal his boy and also gave the scribes ammunition for their unbelief in Christ. That was until the Great Physician came.

The Lord rebukes the unbelief of these disciples – publicly - and the present perverse generation which has no faith; in Matthew 16 verse 4: *"An evil and adulterous generation"*. Any similarities with today's generation?

The Lord`s holy presence provokes the demon which causes the boy to fit. He falls and wallows on the ground, foaming at the mouth. Satan brings us down, leaves us to wallow in our sin and causes a foul mouth. How common is foul speech today!

Jesus in His humanity as a Physician asks a relevant question: *"How long ago is it since this came to him?"* The answer is *"from childhood"*. How important is the development of children! How often sin which becomes established in childhood becomes more serious later. *"He who spares the rod hates his son, but he who loves him disciplines him"* (Proverbs 13 verse 24). This sentiment is echoed in Hebrews 12 verse 5 regarding God`s dealings with us as sons. Discipline is, therefore, part of the Christian growth process but there is no place for abuse. Discipline (chastisement) has a positive beneficial end in view, abuse does not. Politicians seem to have difficulty in distinguishing the two.

Extra facts are now brought to light. He has self-harmed and even attempted suicide when the demon takes over!

The climax of pathos now comes in the father's request: *"If You can do anything, have compassion on us and help us"*. How poignant a request! What desperate need! But he had come to the right person this time; the Lord Jesus, the man of compassion and power.

The Lord turns the father's phrase right round using the same words: "If *you* can – believe ..." It is not a question of the Lord's faith but his. *"All things are possible to him who has faith."* The man is in tears and cries out in desperation: *"I believe, help Thou my unbelief"*. He has faith but is it enough, is it the right kind? He is honest and is still seeking help.

Faith is the key to God - not science. Those who come *"to God must believe that He is, and that He is a rewarder of those who diligently seek Him"* (Hebrews 11 verse 6).

- Faith pleases God: "*without faith it is impossible to please ... God*".

- Faith is the key to Salvation: "*For by grace you have been saved through faith, and that not of yourselves, it is the gift of God*" (Ephesians 2 verse 8).

- Faith is the key to understanding: "*By faith we understand that the worlds were framed by the word of God*" (Hebrews 11 verse 3). Christians know how the world began, why it began, how it is maintained and how it will end, all by faith. What a great privilege!

- Faith has an object: is not an abstract concept or feeling. This man`s faith, although weak, was in Jesus, the "*Author and finisher of faith.*"[127]

He listened to Him and acted upon the information given. He was blessed with his request being answered.

Some people make excuses and say: "I have no faith". Or: "I wish I had faith". How does a person have faith? "*Faith comes by hearing, and hearing by the word of God.*"[128] If a person wishes to have faith, they will read the Bible, the Word of God, which is the basis of faith in God or listen to it preached. They will then be able to follow this man`s example and they will receive the gift of faith.

What of someone who says that they have lost their faith? They need to return to the Word of God which is truth, repent of sin and follow Christ in the fellowship of His church.

Jesus cast out the demon and broke its power, He delivered the boy and saved him, enabling him to hear and speak, lifted him up by the hand and united him quietly to his father.

But not before the demon had a last vindictive throw at the boy, attempting its worst. Its future was sealed in the Abyss and it knew, but the boy was dramatically and gloriously delivered. He could now hear, speak and function normally. The father's faith was strengthened, opposition by the scribes was silenced, the disciples were encouraged to pray and fast and the people saw the majesty of God in this one act of the Lord.

This miracle is unique in that there was a physical result - the epilepsy was gone; a spiritual result in that the demon was removed and a psychological result in that any lunacy effected by the moon was abrogated, and the domestic result was that he was united with his father in peace.

---

[126]Colossians 2 verse 9
[127]Hebrews 12 verse 2
[128]Romans 10 verse 17

The Unusual Case
(The woman who had a spirit of infirmity)

"Now He was teaching in one of the synagogues on the Sabbath. And behold, there was a woman who had a spirit of infirmity eighteen years, and was bent over and could in no way raise herself up. But when Jesus saw her, He called her to Him and said to her, 'Woman, you are loosed from your infirmity'. And He laid His hands on her, and immediately she was made straight, and glorified God. But the ruler of the synagogue answered with indignation, because Jesus had healed on the Sabbath; and he said to the crowd, 'There are six days on which men ought to work; therefore come and be healed on them, and not on the Sabbath day'. The Lord then answered him and said, 'Hypocrite! Does not each one of you on the Sabbath loose his ox or donkey from the stall, and lead it away to water it? So ought not this woman, being a daughter of Abraham, whom Satan has bound — think of it — for eighteen years, be loosed from this bond on the Sabbath?' And when He said these things, all His adversaries were put to shame; and all the multitude rejoiced for all the glorious things that were done by Him."

Luke 13 verses 10-17

This case is so unusual that it could be presented by a Doctor to his colleagues at a Medical Forum as a case of special interest. It is something like this that Luke is doing here to his readers. This miracle of Jesus is only recorded by Luke the Physician. He has a trained eye in observing people and attention to the unusual in the ministry of the Lord Jesus.

It comes after the current news of the accidents and injustices of life and the Lord's comments on them in verses 1-5 of chapter 13 of his Gospel. Accidents don't just happen to the bad. Greater tragedy lies ahead unless people repent, we read.

Next there is the parable of the barren fig tree in verses 6 to 9. Here we see the patience of God becoming exhausted with an unfruitful people. His grace and longsuffering will not always last. Judgment will come unless there is repentance. But He extends grace upon grace in longsuffering before judgment falls.

Now we are introduced to the last record of Jesus' presence in a synagogue. A woman with *"A spirit of infirmity"* is discussed. This seems to be Luke's diagnosis of the lady. He has inquired as to the duration of her condition; 18 long years. He states she was bound by it. That she did not possess an evil spirit would be suggested in the fact that Jesus laid hands on her. He never did this to the demon-possessed. But she was *oppressed* by Satan (verse 16), and bound in spirit, soul and body. 18 years is a long time to have a condition which will not get any better and indeed seems to be getting worse. Hope has gone. She is bent together and can only straighten herself a very little (verse 11). She was held captive by her body.

Was her problem due to an orthopaedic, neurological or metabolic problem or some other condition of the spine such as multiple vertebral fractures, ankylosing spondylitis with fusion of her vertebrae, displacement of vertebrae due to an accident, collapse of spinal vertebrae due to tuberculosis, degenerative osteoarthritis, a dystonic neuromuscular disorder or some other condition?

However, Dr. Herbert Lockyer explains the term *"a spirit of infirmity"* thus: "One of those mysterious derangements of the nervous system having their rise in the mind rather in the body, her physical curvature the consequence of mental obliquity making her melancholy. Her malady was possibly a manifestation of the psyche overruling the soma, resulting in this condition". [129]

Certainly some people use illness as an attention-seeking device and this can become engrained in the psyche leading to a physical condition. Others have manifestations of paralysis in varied parts of the body which are medically deemed "hysterical" or "non-organic" in cause. The common public explanation is that the Doctors don`t know the cause! They do!

The Great Physician, however, certainly knew the cause and the duration of this illness – 18 long years. Her condition was stated as Satanic in origin (verse 16) as Satan was the instigator of the illness no matter the manifestation.

The poor woman is severely handicapped. Her gaze is totally fixed on the earth. She has difficulty with the basics of life; eating, drinking, washing, dressing herself, reaching up or bending down not to mention other basic necessities. Also, she is on the social periphery and religiously she may have been excluded from some of the functions of the synagogue. However, remarkably she still had faith in God no matter the cause and in spite of her condition. Also her presence there that day brought her into permanent blessing.

Although she would not be able to look Jesus in the face due to her problem, she could hear His words. She hears the voice of the Good Shepherd calling to His sheep (verse 12). Perhaps she was in the women's gallery and the Lord called her to Him. He could not go to her, custom would forbid it. He speaks the words no one else could say: *"You are loosed from your infirmity"*. Words of power applied personally and specifically to her need, words that gave her hope and a new mind-set. He then lays His hands on her, both hands. This He did after addressing her as '*Lady*'. The Lord restores again the personal dignity she has lost and gives the comfort, mobility and strength she needed.

The word *'anakupsai'* (lift up) used in verse 11 is said to be used by the ancient Physician Galen of straightening the vertebrae of the spine, according to William Hobart[130] and, in verse 12, the word *'apolelusai'* (are loosed), which is only here used in the New Testament for disease, was used by Medical writers for releasing from disease by relaxing tendons and taking off bandages. In verse 13, the word *'anorthothe'* (she was made straight) was used meaning: "to straighten, to put into natural position abnormal or dislocated parts of the body". Remark has been made by Hobart on the order of the miracle. The relaxing of contracted muscles first, *'apolelusai'*, the removal of the curvature next, *'anorthothe'*, with the restoration of normal position of the spine. Well observed, just as if watching a film in slow motion!

Having restored personal dignity to her, Jesus now announces publicly to the congregation that she is a *"Daughter of Abraham"* (verse 16) thus confirming her faith (Abraham was justified by faith), entitlement to synagogue rites and national inclusion.

This laying on of Jesus` hands confirmed the word to her and reversed the 18 year progression of immobility of the spine in one moment. There was no need of rehab, physiotherapy or psychotherapy. She was healed in a moment and the condition would not recur. The perfect passive tense is used in verse 12. *"The Lord raises them that are bowed down."*[131]

A reading of 1 Corinthians 6 verses 9 to 11 would suggest 'bent', 'twisted', or people apparently fixed in their habits can be 'made straight' if they respond to the word of the Lord. The power of God is available; for the Gospel is *"the power of God unto Salvation for everyone who believes,"*[132] and *"when we were still without strength, in due time Christ died for the ungodly"*.[133] This power brings the power that raised Christ from the dead into a person's life through the Holy Spirit when they believe the gospel.

Also, people who are continually focussed on the things of earth can have their horizons raised to higher, heavenly, things through the word of the Lord.

The human spirit can affect the soul and the body. The Apostle Paul writes to his disciple Timothy: *"For God has not given us a spirit of fear, but of power and of love and of a sound mind"*. [134] He also prays for the Thessalonian Christians: *"May God Himself, the God of peace, sanctify you wholly ("through and through" NIV). May your whole spirit, soul and body be preserved blameless unto the coming of our Lord Jesus Christ"*. [135]

This miracle divided the congregation. The Lord was criticised by the ruler of the synagogue for doing the miracle on the Sabbath day. His answer was simple but conclusive. *"Does not everybody loose his ox or donkey from the stall and lead it to water on the Sabbath day?"* Does a person who is a daughter of Abraham and who has been bound for 18 years by Satan not have greater cause for release on the Sabbath than an animal needing water? As the animal needed water for life, so she needed health for her life to be fulfilled. In releasing her He was breaking the power of Satan. The Ruler's sense of priorities, values and lack of compassion were wrong. Legalism in religion can not only blind leaders but work for Satan!

I have wondered why Jesus healed on the Sabbath day knowing it would upset the Jews. He was, in fact, showing them the real meaning of the Sabbath by bringing people into rest on the day of God's rest. They were sharing in God's rest - what a privilege! The Sabbath was made for man, not man for the Sabbath.

The lady herself is grateful for her deliverance and now straight, lifts up her voice in praise to God. The majority of the congregation recognise the power of the Lord Jesus and glorify God. There is a real "feel good factor" among the people that day. They were glad they had come to church! The adversaries are ashamed of their wrong judgment and lack of concern for the lady in need.

In this woman the Lord fulfils the prophecy of Isaiah 61 verse 1 and His promise of Luke 4 verse 18 to set the captive free. She was captive to Satan and to her own body's limitations. For her, the 'Year of Jubilee', the time of liberty from bondage, had come (see Leviticus 25 verse 10), and she could return to her family now.

This miracle is a picture of the downward drag of a life by Satan. Gradually she became more and more incapacitated and bowed, her eyes more and more focussed on the things of earth, till bound and incapable of freeing herself. But: *"If the Son sets you free, you shall be free indeed"*.[136] She was made free - are you free?

The causes of illness are sometimes sin as in the man in John 5; sometimes Satan as here and sometimes unknown to us as in the case of the man born blind in John 9. Sometimes there are atrocities committed by people and sometimes accidents happen as in Luke 13 verses 1 to 4. We live in a fallen world but the early believers were described as: *"Those who turned the world upside down"*,[137] or really the right way up! This still happens when the gospel is preached and believed today.

---

[129]Lockyer Herbert, *"All the Miracles of the Bible"*, page 223.
[130]Hobart W, *"The Medical Language of Luke"*, pages 21 and 22.
[131]Psalm 146 verse 8
[132]Romans 1 verse 16
[133]Romans 5 verse 6
[134]2 Timothy 1 verse 7
[135]1 Thessalonians 5 verse 23
[136]John 8 verse 36
[137]Acts 17 verse 6

The Medical Case
(The man with dropsy)

"Now it happened, as He went into the house of one of the rulers of the Pharisees to eat bread on the Sabbath, that they watched Him closely. And behold, there was a certain man before Him who had dropsy. And Jesus, answering, spoke to the lawyers and Pharisees, saying, 'Is it lawful to heal on the Sabbath?' But they kept silent. And He took him and healed him, and let him go. Then He answered them, saying, 'Which of you, having a donkey or an ox that has fallen into a pit, will not immediately pull him out on the Sabbath day?' And they could not answer Him regarding these things."

Luke 14 verses 1-6

This miracle is only recorded by Luke the Beloved Physician. It is the seventh miracle performed by the Lord on the Sabbath day. It was not performed in the synagogue this time but in a house. Not an ordinary house but that of an important Pharisee. What was the motive in the invitation given to Jesus? Was it friendliness, a sense of duty in giving hospitality to a famous Rabbi or was it a 'set up' to trap the Saviour? It seems it may have been the latter as, in verse 1, we read: *"They were watching him"*. According to Professor William Barclay, the word translated "watching" is used for "interested and sinister espionage. Jesus was under scrutiny".[138] Also, Norman Crawford points out[139] the periphrastic imperfect tense of the word *'paratereo'* with the middle voice in Greek means they, the Pharisees, were out to trap the Saviour.

'Dropsy' is the old-fashioned word for water retention (oedema), causing swelling of tissues due to medical conditions such as heart failure. Kidney disease (nephrotic syndrome), liver disease, thyroid disease (myxoedema), some lung diseases and obstruction of the lymphatic system may be other causes. Swelling occurs in the spaces between body tissues and under the skin. It is not usually an acute condition.

My picture of this man is of a person with a swollen abdomen and legs, having reduced mobility due to the swelling and sitting in a semi-upright position for personal comfort in front of Jesus, in a prominent place in the room. His Eastern clothing would hide some of his symptoms but all would be perceived by Jesus and He would know the severity of his condition.

According to Celsus, a Physician at the time of Jesus: "Dropsy is least alarming when commenced without being preceded by any disease ... but if caused by an acute disease is seldom conducted to cure". This man was physically in deep trouble but what a 'coincidence' that he was present at the right time in front of the Saviour!

Jesus takes the initiative on this occasion and proceeds to silence the Pharisees and lawyers, experts in the Law. His question was on the legitimacy of the healing He was about to do on the Sabbath day. He then heals the man and reasons in verse 5 that the rescue of a man is surely more important than the rescue of an animal, which was allowed by Jewish Law on the Sabbath day.[140] They, in their blindness, had never evaluated this comparison with reference to a person's well-being on the Sabbath, nor had they imbibed the teaching of the Lord recorded in Matthew 12 verses 10 to 14 when *they* challenged Him with the question of the Law regarding the healing of the man with the withered hand on the Sabbath. The Lord showed at that time that it was lawful to do good on the Sabbath. Their priorities and concept of the nature of God was all wrong. Jesus was not breaking the Sabbath at all. Not only was healing justified but the man's condition was deserving of emergency attention in the assessment of Jesus – verse 5. Anyone who has observed or experienced this condition would heartily agree. Also, he may have had breathing difficulties.

According to David Stern[141] modern 'halakhah' has a three-fold division of permissible healing on the Sabbath:

1   to save life is a duty,
2   caring for the seriously ill is allowed within constraints
3   treating minor ailments is prohibited by rabbinical decree as they require grinding to prepare the medicine.

What was the legal opinion of the chief Pharisees and lawyers regarding this man's condition? If they looked upon the man as seriously ill, then they had no argument with the Lord's healing on the Sabbath as per 1 and 2 above. If they considered it minor, He did not use medicine in treatment, so again they had no argument with him as per 3 above.

Jesus, however, did not employ rabbinical law to the case in point. He knew the Law of Moses better than the Lawyers and Pharisees but lived and practised not only the letter but also the spirit of the Law. *"The Lord is well pleased for His righteousness' sake; He will exalt the law and make it honourable"* says Isaiah[142] demonstrating here the true righteousness of the Law. The ingrained legalistic thinking of the Rabbis was well short in the glory of God. The Lord here turned the tables on His enemies who had set up this sick man as a case to bring public condemnation on Him.

Jesus took the man, healed him immediately and *"let him go"*. It reads so simple! Yet the cause *and* the symptoms are healed at once. But the immediate cure of such a condition should be followed by the passing of considerable amount of urine. This is a controlled procedure for medical reasons. Hence the Lord is, in the miracle, including the aftercare in His treatment.

He was a prisoner to his condition of water retention (oedema) and unable to help himself, just as an animal in a well (of water) would have been unable to help itself. In this analogy, the Lord uses the case of the rescue of the ass or ox on the Sabbath day and shows by *'a fortiori'* comparison the absurdity of their argument and the reason for His intervention.

Dr Herbert Lockyer seems to see a connection with the woman in the previous chapter, Luke 13 verses 15 and 16, who was bowed for 18 years and delivered by Jesus. [143] She was loosed from the binding of her fixed joints just as the ox or ass was loosed from the tethering of the stall and taken to water to drink (verse 15) on the Sabbath day. Likewise here, the man with dropsy is likened to the animal rescued from a well. If left alone, he would drown in his body water. He needed immediate rescue like the animal in the well. Hence the Lord Jesus, the Great Physician, came to his rescue by freeing him.

It is interesting that this miracle is followed in Luke, who loves moral order in his writings, by remarks on those who were swollen with self-importance and pride, scrambling for the seats of honour in the house.

We also need to rid ourselves of anything which could be making us 'swell'. It may be pride, self-importance, false self-image, wealth, position, education and such.

We are enjoined to have the same thinking as He who was meek and lowly in heart, who also humbled Himself to become a servant *"even to the death of the cross"* (Philippians 2 verse 8). Anything we have, we have received from God.

---

[138] William Barclay, *"The Gospel of Luke"*, page 222
[139] 'Luke' by Norman Crawford in *"What the Bible Teaches"* series, page 242
[140] Exodus 21 verse 33
[141] David Stern, *"Jewish New Testament Commentary"*, page 117
[142] Isaiah 42 verse 21
[143] Dr Herbert Lockyer, *"All the Miracles of the Bible"*, page 226

The Case of Communal Disease
(The ten men who were lepers)

"Now it happened as He went to Jerusalem that He passed through the midst of Samaria and Galilee. Then as He entered a certain village, there met Him ten men who were lepers, who stood afar off. And they lifted up their voices and said, 'Jesus, Master, have mercy on us!' So when He saw them, He said to them, 'Go, show yourselves to the priests'. And so it was that as they went, they were cleansed. And one of them, when he saw that he was healed, returned, and with a loud voice glorified God, and fell down on his face at His feet, giving Him thanks. And he was a Samaritan. So Jesus answered and said, 'Were there not ten cleansed? But where are the nine? Were there not any found who returned to give glory to God except this foreigner?' And He said to him, 'Arise, go your way. Your faith has made you well.'"

Luke 17 verses 11-19

It is said that the Second World War saw the best community spirit and co-operation of people in the United Kingdom for generations. Adversity brings together and unites. There was a common enemy, and a spirit of sharing with those in need developed. Such was the case here. The common enemy was not war but Leprosy. Jews, who had no time for Samaritans, are living together with them and sharing life as brother lepers in isolation, hardship and suffering. Some cases of leprosy would be more advanced than others, but the strong would help the weak in such community living, even up till death.

The Lord is going up to Jerusalem again. This time the Samaritans allow Him to pass through their territory, unlike the prohibition of Luke 10 when a Samaritan village forbad Him, invoking the wrath of the Sons of Thunder, James and John, who display a spirit of intolerance, racism, even revenge and murder! How dare these heretics refuse their Master transit!

At this village the Lord Jesus encounters ten lepers *"who stood afar off"*, a little community of the sick in isolation.[144] Unlike the leper of Chapter 5, they do not approach the Lord but keep their distance and shout out calling: *"Jesus, Master"*, and ask for mercy.[145] They obviously knew who He was and had some kind of faith in Him. His answer on seeing them was: *"Go, show yourselves to the priests"*. They unitedly obey and were cleansed as they were going. Only one returned, and falling on his face in appreciation for his cleansing, gave thanks to the Saviour with a loud voice. He had lifted his voice with the other nine loudly in need, now his was a sole voice in thanksgiving.

The Lord remarks on the lack of appreciation and failure of the other nine to glorify God, emphasising that this man was a foreigner, a Samaritan. He simply asked for mercy, received it and was grateful for it. This patient went away in the blessing of total healing and salvation by faith in Christ. How like the nine we often are! We ask God in need but so often forget to return to give thanks. One of the features of 'the last days' is lack of appreciation (2 Timothy 3 verse 2). People should be thankful. We depend on God for everything; our breath, our health, our food, our clothes, our warmth, our very existence.

It used to be that people with an infectious disease in Scotland were isolated in a "Fever Hospital" or Infectious Disease Hospital; an isolated community away from the local towns. A similarity can be seen in this story by Luke, the Physician. They were isolated according to the Law and lived in a community of the sick.

This miracle of a community of lepers being healed is remarkable in certain features. They all had the same disease. They were united in need. They had a united approach to Jesus, requesting mercy, all calling Him '*Master*'. They were united in faith; they believed He could cure them now and they all obeyed at once. They all went off to the priests, even the Samaritan(s)! The ten would be all cleansed at once as they were in the process of going to the priests. But one was different, he returned to give thanks.

In this miracle, we see one command of the Lord healing ten people at once! One word healed the varied stages of leprosy in ten people. This was based on His mercy to all. This was the need of all. They could not heal themselves and no one else could. They were really in various stages of an incurable disease.

Jesus, a Jew, again commends a Samaritan. Not as in a parable as the parable of the 'Good Samaritan', but the present stranger who returned. Luke as a Physician dealing with people, in his Gospel notes the outcast, the homeless, the despised, the widow and the stranger. The Lord Himself was recorded by Luke as a stranger. He who had been a refugee in Egypt as a child was homeless in His latter ministry and treated as an outsider by His own Nation, the Nation of Israel. Finally, in being crucified outside the gates of Jerusalem He was treated as a leper by it. He understood their feeling of rejection and isolation.

It would have astonished the priests to see so many lepers, cleansed at once, coming to them for the Ceremony of the Law of the Leper![146] Would they be too late at this stage of Christ's ministry to recognise this miracle as vindicating Him as Messiah? And were there any other Samaritans in the group obeying the word of Jesus by going to the Jewish priests as well as the Jews? Or did the Samaritan quoted in Scripture turn back to give thanks to the Lord instead of going to the priests or did he go to the Jewish priests after returning to give thanks? He obviously put his Saviour first, no matter the sequences of events, worshipping at His feet.

The result of this miracle must have had disturbing repercussions in the local communities. Long-absent sick relatives suddenly returning home cured of a diagnosed incurable disease! This would upset the routine of families. Some would be delighted that a loved one had returned home cleansed, but others would resent the status quo being disturbed. One has witnessed the latter with men who had long absences due to a career in Naval Service returning home on retirement being resented, side-lined, ignored, even divorced! The same could apply with other Service personnel or long-term prisoners coming home after release. It may have been the order for relatives to visit and leave food at the site of the leper colony, but this was now a domestic and social issue causing upheaval. Some may have had no home to go to, life moves on; from a company of homeless exiles to perhaps home isolation. Also, for the cleansed lepers, it would also be difficult for *them* to adjust to new life of close family relationships after long absence from home.

The fact that Luke records them as standing '*afar off*' shows they were obeying the Law of Moses (Leviticus 13 verse 46 and Numbers 5 verse 2).

This phrase '*afar off*' or '*great way off*' used by Luke (AV and NKJV) reminds us:

- Of the publican (tax collector) of Luke 18 who stood in the Temple at Jerusalem '*afar off*' begging the mercy of God. He felt his guilt before a Holy God. His spiritual eye was on the blood shed for atonement on the mercy seat of the Ark of the Covenant in the Most Holy place. He needed *justification* from God (Romans 3 verse 25; 5 verse 9).

- The prodigal son in Luke 15 was seen by his father '*while he was a great way off*'. He was in rebellion, he needed *reconciliation* to his father (Romans 5 verse 10).

- This leper who with others stood '*afar off*' was unclean. He needed *cleansing* (Leviticus 16 verse 30; Psalm 51 verse 2; Zechariah 13 verse 1; Hebrews 9 verse 14; 1 John 1 verse 9).

All sin leads to us being 'afar off' from God, hence we need to be brought near in reconciliation, first of all to God, then to one another. This is achieved not by human effort but through the shed blood of Jesus at the cross of Calvary (Ephesians 2 verses 13-18).

It is noteworthy that the leper community that was united in need is now separated in Salvation! All were blessed physically in cleansing but only one blessed spiritually. Only he is a candidate for God's New Community, the Church, 'God's Alternative Society'.

What disease or condition with comparative opprobrium to leprosy has stigma and could exclude a person from society today? No sin is greater than the work of Christ on the cross. Such a person, if they came to the Lord Jesus in repentance and faith, would be cleansed and accepted by Him and become suitable for fellowship in a local church, whose members they would need for support.

It may be of significance that there were ten lepers. The number ten is usually taken as representing man's responsibility to God but it is often associated negatively in a community setting:

- there were not 10 righteous men in Sodom
- there were 10 plagues in Egypt
- there are ten 'nots' in the 10 commandments
- ten spies gave an evil report of Canaan
- ten times the Children of Israel tempted God in the Wilderness
- it took Naomi in the book of Ruth ten years to decide to return to Israel.

In Matthew 14 verse 35 and Mark 6 verses 53-56, many people from their homes in the town and country are brought to Jesus and placed in the streets so that they might reach out and *"just touch the hem of His garment. And as many as touched Him were made well"*. This is a different type of community healing; individual yet multiple in a specific area.

It is reminiscent also of the many healings in Capernaum in the house of Peter in Mark 1. But the above miracle is outdoors and public without individual consultation with Jesus, the Great Physician.

The virtue of Christ alone is again seen to be sufficient as in the case of the woman with the issue of blood when virtue went out of the Saviour to heal. He felt His power go out of Him on that occasion - how much more must the instantaneous healing of the ten have cost Him! He has infinite resources.

---

[103]Harrison R.K. in the *"International Standard Bible Encyclopaedia"*, 1986, says all Leprosy in the New Testament is Hansen's Disease i.e. true Leprosy.

The fact that the ten lepers lived in isolation would suggest they had a contagious form of the disease. Leprosy nowadays in the East, such as in Ethiopia or India, is not contagious but may be passed on in families or to those in close contact if nutrition is bad or poor housing conditions. As has been the case of Tuberculosis in the West, Leprosy bacterium probably has attenuated over the years.

The Surgical Case
(The right ear of the high priest's servant)
(Body Part Replacement)

"And while He was still speaking, behold, a multitude; and he who was called Judas, one of the twelve, went before them and drew near to Jesus to kiss Him. But Jesus said to him, 'Judas, are you betraying the Son of Man with a kiss?' When those around Him saw what was going to happen, they said to Him, 'Lord, shall we strike with the sword?' And one of them struck the servant of the high priest and cut off his right ear. But Jesus answered and said, 'Permit even this'. And He touched his ear and healed him. Then Jesus said to the chief priests, captains of the temple, and the elders who had come to Him, 'Have you come out, as against a robber, with swords and clubs? When I was with you daily in the temple, you did not try to seize Me. But this is your hour, and the power of darkness.'"

Luke 22 verses 47-53

"When Jesus had spoken these words, He went out with His disciples over the Brook Kidron, where there was a garden, which He and His disciples entered. And Judas, who betrayed Him, also knew the place; for Jesus often met there with His disciples. Then Judas, having received a detachment of troops, and officers from the chief priests and Pharisees, came there with lanterns, torches, and weapons. Jesus therefore, knowing all things that would come upon Him, went forward and said to them, 'Whom are you seeking?' They answered Him, 'Jesus of Nazareth'. Jesus said to them, 'I am He'. And Judas, who betrayed Him, also stood with them. Now when He said to them, 'I am He', they drew back and fell to the

ground. Then He asked them again, 'Whom are you seeking?' And they said, 'Jesus of Nazareth'. Jesus answered, 'I have told you that I am He. Therefore, if you seek Me, let these go their way', that the saying might be fulfilled which He spoke, 'Of those whom You gave Me I have lost none'. Then Simon Peter, having a sword, drew it and struck the high priest's servant, and cut off his right ear. The servant's name was Malchus. So Jesus said to Peter, 'Put your sword into the sheath. Shall I not drink the cup which My Father has given Me?'"

John 18 verses 1-11

This is the last miracle of the Lord Jesus before His death and is recorded in all four Gospels, thus signifying its importance. It is the only surgical miracle performed by Jesus in the Gospels and involves not a removal as in most surgery but restoration of a body part. It is also the restoration of a disciple's wrong.

"Then I restored that which I took not away" was prophesied of Messiah in Psalm 69 verse 4. Here this is seen in a physical way as well as being primarily applicable to the Lord`s unique saving work on the cross. The spiritual restoration of Simon Peter who caused the injury would come later.

The disciples were with Him in the garden of Gethsemane, armed with two swords. John tells us that Peter had one. We don`t know who had the other. When Judas led the hostile band armed with clubs and swords into the garden, the disciples now alert, discerned what was about to happen and asked permission from the Lord to use the swords. But before an answer came, Peter sprang to defend his Master, drew his sword and lopped off the ear of the High Priest`s servant. John, who seemed to be acquaint with the High Priest's household, tells us that it was the right ear of Malchus, a servant of the High Priest of Israel (John 18 verse 10). This is the only servant named in the New Testament. If Peter had killed him, it would have been national news!

Had Peter been awake in the garden earlier when the Lord was praying, he may have had a different approach to the situation by hearing: *"Not My will but Thine be done"* (Luke 22 verse 42). Also, he was advised to pray in preparation for testing (verse 46).

Consider the consequences if Peter had been more accurate with his sword. He would have been arrested by the soldiers present and subsequently put to death for his attempt on the life of the High Priest's servant. He may indeed have died with his Lord (Matthew 26 verse 5)! Who then would use the keys of the kingdom in the future? Also, the Lord would have been open to the accusation that He was not able to control, never mind save, His own disciples.

Peter's action was outwith the Divine plan and could have caused uproar and bloodshed in the capital thus seemingly justifying the argument of the High Priest, chief priests and elders of the Jews that Jesus and His disciples were a danger to national peace. Roman retribution would ensue on the very disciples the Lord was protecting: *"If you seek Me, let these go their way"* (John 18 verse 8). That was to say nothing of the possible death, humanly speaking, of Messiah - **not** according to the Scriptures (1 Corinthians 15 verse 3). But three times in his Gospel John records the personal prophecy of Jesus: *"The Son of Man must be lifted up"*.

The Lord immediately healed the raw ear of Malchus with His touch (Luke 22 verse 51) and restored the damage done by His loyal but misguided disciple. The touch of power to heal an enemy! Mercy and care shown to the very man who was sent to arrest Him! The super-abundant grace of Christ!

Jesus rebuked His zealous disciple reminding him not only that He had the immediate availability of the angelic armies of heaven at one command but also the purpose for which He had come: *"How then would the Scriptures be fulfilled that say it must happen in this way?"* (Matthew 26 verses 52-54 NIV). "Suffer ye thus far" (Luke 22 verse

51) shows the Lord's willingness to be taken, a request that His captors free His arms to allow the healing[147], as well as a rebuke to Peter.

In this last recorded miracle of the Lord before the cross, we see once more His healing touch. At the beginning of the Gospel of Luke, the Lord touches the incurable Leper, at the end of the Gospel, He touches the incurable ear of a servant. In the book of Revelation, the glorified Christ wants to touch the ear of the faithful in the churches and have them hear what the Spirit is saying: "*He who has an ear, let him hear*". So many have stopped ears, He is appealing to the few, just as today.

In Chapter 22 verse 43, Luke tells us of the weakness of the Lord in the garden of Gethsemane and the ministry of an angel from Heaven to strengthen Him. He is seen as: "*A little lower than the angels ...*" (Hebrews 2 verse 7). Now, in the same garden, we see His power in healing the ear of Malchus: "*Having become so much better than the angels ...*" (Hebrews 1 verse 4). "What manner of man is this?" Between these two events it is recorded that He prayed.

This episode in the garden made a deep impression on John. He describes the scene in Chapter 18 verse 2, Peter's action with the sword in verse 10, and notes that he did himself no favours (verse 26) for we read that the kinsman of Malchus recognised him later when by the fire in the courtyard of the High Priest`s House. This led to Peter's third denial and the cock crow as prophesied by the Lord. How our mistakes return to haunt us! What great danger to use human weapons for spiritual ends!

But it is interesting to note that the relative of Malchus only mentions the presence of Peter in the garden, not the incident of the attempted murder by him! Was this because the healing was so quickly and perfectly done by the Lord?

Why was John, who also was in the garden, not identified in the High Priest's house as a fellow disciple? Speculation has been made that he supplied the High Priest's household with fish from Galilee when in his father Zebedee's business and was thus accepted as a legitimate visitor, not a suspect; apocryphal but interesting. No matter, it is generally accepted that John was acquainted with the High Priest.

We may cut someone's ear off metaphorically by what we say or by our attitude so that person does not listen to our witness again. It takes a miracle of the Lord to restore it.

Both Luke and John clearly state the ear was cut off. For restoration of such an injury today, the severed ear would have been searched for, carefully wrapped in a clean damp cloth if available and taken to the Casualty Department at the local hospital. A Plastic Surgeon would be summoned and a delicate operation performed under aseptic conditions using microsurgical techniques. Even then, there would be no guarantee of success.

In the healing of the ear of this man, however, we see body part replacement, a creative act of the Lord and a restorative act. As mentioned, this is the only 'surgical miracle' recorded in the Gospels. It shows The Great Physician is also The Great Creator and The Great Restorer. He can create from nothing a new ear to suit an adult body, a mirror image of the other on the appropriate side; with size, shape and function in a moment and attach it by a touch without instruments, stitches or staples under the Paschal night sky with flickering light from torches and lanterns!

What of the restoration of perfect hearing? Textbooks on the anatomy of the ear, neurophysiology, audiology, if consulted, will display the wonder of this act of mercy performed in a moment.

I wonder what the thoughts of this servant would be after the crucifixion and resurrection of his Surgeon? Or did he even have a second thought? Such is the heart of man.

The One who healed an ear here is also the One who advised surgery of the right eye and right hand in His teaching of self-discipline in Matthew 5 verses 29 and 30!

The Three Cases of the Dead being Raised
(Jairus' daughter, the widow of Nain's son and Lazarus)

"No one ever came back to tell us", a lady said to me when discussing what happens after death. Well, she is wrong! There are three fully-documented cases in the New Testament where Jesus raised the dead with witnesses present. Also, He raised Himself from the dead. This is something no Physician has ever done. He Himself, the Great Physician, never lost a patient and death was no barrier to His power.

JAIRUS' DAUGHTER
A Dramatic Paediatric Case

"While He spoke these things to them, behold, a ruler came and worshipped Him, saying, 'My daughter has just died, but come and lay Your hand on her and she will live'. So Jesus arose and followed him, and so did His disciples. And suddenly, a woman who had a flow of blood for twelve years came from behind and touched the hem of His garment. For she said to herself, 'If only I may touch His garment, I shall be made well'. But Jesus turned around, and when He saw her He said, 'Be of good cheer, daughter; your faith has made you well'. And the woman was made well from that hour. When Jesus came into the ruler's house, and saw the flute players and the noisy crowd wailing, He said to them, 'Make room, for the girl is not dead, but sleeping'. And they ridiculed Him. But when the crowd was put outside, He went in and took her by the hand, and the girl arose. And the report of this went out into all that land."

Matthew 9 verses 18-26

"Now when Jesus had crossed over again by boat to the other side, a great multitude gathered to Him; and He was by the sea. And behold, one of the rulers of the synagogue came, Jairus by name. And when he saw Him, he fell at His feet and begged Him earnestly, saying, 'My little daughter lies at the point of death. Come and lay Your hands on her, that she may be healed, and she will live.' So Jesus went with him, and a great multitude followed Him and thronged Him. Now a certain woman had a flow of blood for twelve years, and had suffered many things from many physicians. She had spent all that she had and was no better, but rather grew worse. When she heard about Jesus, she came behind Him in the crowd and touched His garment. For she said, 'If only I may touch His clothes, I shall be made well'. Immediately the fountain of her blood was dried up, and she felt in her body that she was healed of the affliction. And Jesus, immediately knowing in Himself that power had gone out of Him, turned around in the crowd and said, 'Who touched My clothes?' But His disciples said to Him, 'You see the multitude thronging You, and You say, "Who touched Me?"'" And He looked around to see her who had done this thing. But the woman, fearing and trembling, knowing what had happened to her, came and fell down before Him and told Him the whole truth. And He said to her, 'Daughter, your faith has made you well. Go in peace, and be healed of your affliction.' While He was still speaking, some came from the ruler of the synagogue's house who said, 'Your daughter is dead. Why trouble the Teacher any further?' As soon as Jesus heard the word that was spoken, He said to the ruler of the synagogue, 'Do not be afraid; only believe'. And He permitted no one to follow Him except Peter, James, and John the brother of James. Then He came to the house of the ruler of the synagogue, and saw a tumult and those who wept and wailed loudly. When He came in, He said to them, 'Why make this commotion and weep? The child is not dead, but sleeping'. And they ridiculed Him. But when He had put them all outside, He took the father and the mother of the child, and those who were with Him, and entered where the child was lying. Then

He took the child by the hand, and said to her, 'Talitha, cumi', which is translated, 'Little girl, I say to you, arise'. Immediately the girl arose and walked, for she was twelve years of age. And they were overcome with great amazement. But He commanded them strictly that no one should know it, and said that something should be given her to eat."

Mark 5 verses 21-43

"So it was, when Jesus returned, that the multitude welcomed Him, for they were all waiting for Him. And behold, there came a man named Jairus, and he was a ruler of the synagogue. And he fell down at Jesus' feet and begged Him to come to his house, for he had an only daughter about twelve years of age, and she was dying. But as He went, the multitudes thronged Him. Now a woman, having a flow of blood for twelve years, who had spent all her livelihood on physicians and could not be healed by any, came from behind and touched the border of His garment. And immediately her flow of blood stopped. And Jesus said, 'Who touched Me?' When all denied it, Peter and those with him said, 'Master, the multitudes throng and press You, and You say, "Who touched Me?"' But Jesus said, 'Somebody touched Me, for I perceived power going out from Me'. Now when the woman saw that she was not hidden, she came trembling; and falling down before Him, she declared to Him in the presence of all the people the reason she had touched Him and how she was healed immediately. And He said to her, 'Daughter, be of good cheer; your faith has made you well. Go in peace.' While He was still speaking, someone came from the ruler of the synagogue's house, saying to him, 'Your daughter is dead. Do not trouble the Teacher.' But when Jesus heard it, He answered him, saying, 'Do not be afraid; only believe, and she will be made well.' When He came into the house, He permitted no one to go in except Peter, James, and John, and the father and mother of the girl. Now all wept and mourned for her; but He said, 'Do not weep; she is not dead, but sleeping'. And they ridiculed Him, knowing that she was dead. But He put them all outside, took her

by the hand and called, saying, 'Little girl, arise'. Then her spirit returned, and she arose immediately. And He commanded that she be given something to eat. And her parents were astonished, but He charged them to tell no one what had happened."

Luke 8 verses 41-56

The fact that Jesus raised a young girl from death in a house in Galilee is recorded in no less than three Gospels; Matthew 9, Mark 5, and Luke 8. The father of the girl was an important man in the local community, a ruler of the synagogue, named Jairus. He came and implored Jesus to come and help when she was not just severely ill, but dying. But by the time Jesus reached the house the young girl had already died. Some think she may have just been unconscious. But Jairus' servant said she was dead, the mourners said she was dead and they laughed Jesus to scorn because they considered themselves experts at the business of death and funerals. The reference by the Lord to her sleeping is, I believe, figurative, as is also the same phrase spoken in reference to sleep in the case of Lazarus who had been dead at least two days at that point. The Lord gently took the young girl by the hand and said: *"Young girl, I am speaking to you, arise."*[148] Immediately, her spirit returned,[149] she got up and walked about in perfect health and strength as if she had never been ill or had died. She must have been off her food before her death as the Lord ordered that she should be given something to eat!

This miracle so impressed Mark that he retains the Aramaic language spoken by Jesus in Galilee, *Talitha cumi* which is variously translated: *"Little lamb, arise"*,[150] "My child, get up" (NIV), *"Little girl, I say to you arise"* (NKJV). The Lord here in this gentle command penetrates the kingdom of death, specifically revives the spirit of this little girl, unites it with her body and addresses her personality. Mark notes she was twelve years of age; Luke that she was an only child. So much potential is lost in a young person's death.

Mark also records in verse 36 ("*parakousas ton logon laloumenon*"), that Jesus overheard, (or disregarded), the advice of the people who were from Jairus` house telling him the sad news of her death. This action would fulfil the Prophecy of Isaiah 42 verse 19: "*Who is ... deaf as My messenger whom I send?*" Observe Jesus, the Servant of Jehovah, in action! He is not stumbled by the sad news of her death but from His own faith encourages the faith of Jairus to rise further than the confidence he already had in His ability to heal. He can also raise the dead. "*Be not afraid, only believe*", the Lord says. "*A bruised reed He will not break, and smoking flax He will not quench.*" [151] Faith and fear are mutually exclusive.

The Lord had removed the unbelievers who mocked Him and took in the three disciples of faith with Him into the house; Peter, James and John. Peter, would in future raise the dead, let him learn lessons here. Remove unbelief, only work with a minor in the presence of a parent or guardian, be sensitive, fulfil the human aspect of the work before the Divine operates.

The parents would be witnesses along with the disciples to this miracle. The atmosphere was now conducive to the Saviour's working. Any Physician or Surgeon would seek such calm before a delicate procedure, much more so the operation of raising a child to life.

All three Gospels note the funeral customs prior to burial had been in progress. This was a bodily resurrection of a dead young girl and her restoration to her parents.

On this occasion, the favoured three disciples saw resurrection at the closest of quarters reported in the New Testament.

WIDOW OF NAIN'S SON
The Case of Home and Community Restoration
"*Now it happened, the day after, that He went into a city called*

*Nain; and many of His disciples went with Him, and a large crowd.
And when He came near the gate of the city, behold, a dead man was
being carried out, the only son of his mother; and she was a widow.
And a large crowd from the city was with her. When the Lord saw
her, He had compassion on her and said to her, 'Do not weep'. Then
He came and touched the open coffin, and those who carried him
stood still. And He said, 'Young man, I say to you, arise'. So he
who was dead sat up and began to speak. And He presented him to
his mother. Then fear came upon all, and they glorified God, saying,
'A great prophet has risen up among us'; and, 'God has visited His
people'. And this report about Him went throughout all Judea and
all the surrounding region."*

Luke 7 verses 11-17

This first fully recorded raising of the dead by the Lord Jesus
occurred in the village of Nain, a village on the West slopes of the
Jezreel valley with an extensive and commanding view. The word
'Nain' means 'pleasant', which the Jewish Rabbis saw as a fulfilment
of the prophecy concerning this part of the land by Jacob to his
son Issachar: "*He saw ... that the land was pleasant*".[152] There is still
a small village there today with an Arab population. It is a spot at
present where tour buses stop on the way to Tiberius from Tel Aviv
for passenger refreshment. It is about six miles from Nazareth,
North West of the hill 'Little Hermon' and 25 miles South West from
Capernaum. Eusebius, the early Church Father, noted it is near
Endor where King Saul consulted a witch before his doom at the
battle with the Philistines.[153] Here Jesus, the promised King of Israel,
will presently bring blessing to a widow woman by raising her son.

This miracle is only recorded by the Physician Luke. He would
have seen many deaths but never in his career a resurrection! This
was a young man lying in his open coffin or bier, probably made of
wickerwork, on the way to burial. Leading the procession would be
the women, a Galilean custom, and accompanying the procession
would be the sound of flutes, cymbals, even trumpets and the

lamentations by the women. The bier would be carried by unshod friends[154] and neighbours exchanging roles to share the 'good work' of escorting the dead to burial. Many of the town people accompanied the bier observing Jewish law and custom[155] but also demonstrating the popularity of the widow and the sympathy they had for her. This was a doubly sad occasion as this was the only son of the widow, notes Luke in his Gospel. It was her second bereavement. Her hope for her future comfort and security had gone in his death. Also, perhaps a shift in the future inheritance of her land according to the ancient Law of Israel.[156]

However, another procession met this one on its way to the tomb, a band of hope. Jesus, His disciples and a crowd of followers coming up from Capernaum via Endor converge on the mourners. Seeing the sorrow of the widow evoked compassion by the Son of Mary on the one who is bereft of her only son. The Lord says not the usual Rabbinical: "Weep with them, all ye who are bitter in heart", nor does He reverently follow the bier with His disciples to the grave as per custom but tenderly says: *"Don`t cry anymore"*. He stimulates hope.

He touches the coffin (not the young man). He is a Jewish Rabbi ministering to the lost sheep of Israel and avoided ceremonial defilement even although He as the Holy One could not be defiled. The mourners stop. Some think the rock-carved tombs to the West of the town was the intended destiny of the mourners, others the unfenced burying ground to the East. No matter, they would await a different prisoner as the Lord of life will exercise His strength in resurrection. He says: "Young man, I am speaking to *you*, get up". He sits up,[157] alive, and begins to speak! His personality as well as his life had returned! He is a talker! What did he say? We are not told. The Prince of Life delivers him to his mother. The concept in *"delivered"* (KJV) suggests - from the power of death. The word *"presented"* in the NKVJ paints a lovely picture of the act of giving an acceptable present. The word in the original Greek is indeed *"gave"*, surely a wonderful gift from God the Son to this lady bereaved of her son. The crowd acclaim that God has visited His people.[158] In secular Greek, the word *'visited'* was used of a physician visiting the sick. The Lord Jesus, the Great Physician, had indeed visited the sick and raised him up, not just to health but to life.

What a reunion! What a miracle! Later in this very chapter, when sending proof of His credentials to John Baptist, Jesus includes the statement: *"The dead are raised"*. This gave the people hope as they glorify God, having seen in the miracle the presence of God among His people. This revelation exceeds the personal and local aspect of the miracle to Nain, a remote Galilean town. God is among His people in the Christ, His Son. How we estimate is often by the big event with big numbers. God often uses the small, the unknown, the weak to glorify Himself. What was the boy's name? What was his mother`s name? We are not told. But we know this was a "Nain" – "a most pleasant" – event.

It naturally became news which reached John Baptist in prison. Hence the ensuing enquiry by him as to the Divine timing of Jesus' plans. He has doubts. Perhaps he is thinking: "Why am I in prison if Messiah has come and has such authority?" John must have forgotten his own public statement: *"He must increase, I must decrease"*. The Messenger is to give place to the Message, the Voice to the Word, the Herald to the King. He has fulfilled his commission. The highway has been prepared for Israel's God. The Lord upholds publicly the character, place and power of John. He is the greatest born of women, but he that is least in the Kingdom of God is greater than he! The believer today in the Kingdom is greater than John? Surely this must be positional privilege for us as we are part of the Bride of Christ. John was the best man – *"the friend of the bridegroom"*, he introduced the Bridegroom. Noticeably, Jesus gives these compliments of John *after* John's disciples had left. John would never hear this public praise by Jesus. His reward would be left till the resurrection of the just.

LAZARUS
The Case of Treating a Friend

"Now a certain man was sick, Lazarus of Bethany, the town of Mary and her sister Martha. It was that Mary who anointed the Lord with fragrant oil and wiped His feet with her hair, whose brother Lazarus was sick. Therefore the sisters sent to Him, saying, 'Lord, behold, he whom You love is sick'. When Jesus heard that, He said, 'This sickness is not unto death, but for the glory of God, that the Son of God may be glorified through it'. Now Jesus loved Martha and her sister and Lazarus. So, when He heard that he was sick, He stayed two more days in the place where He was. Then after this He said to the disciples, 'Let us go to Judea again'. The disciples said to Him, 'Rabbi, lately the Jews sought to stone You, and are You going there again?' Jesus answered, 'Are there not twelve hours in the day? If anyone walks in the day, he does not stumble, because he sees the light of this world. But if one walks in the night, he stumbles, because the light is not in him.' These things He said, and after that He said to them, 'Our friend Lazarus sleeps, but I go that I may wake him up'. Then His disciples said, 'Lord, if he sleeps he will get well'. However, Jesus spoke of his death, but they thought that He was speaking about taking rest in sleep. Then Jesus said to them plainly, 'Lazarus is dead. And I am glad for your sakes that I was not there, that you may believe. Nevertheless let us go to him.' Then Thomas, who is called the Twin, said to his fellow disciples, 'Let us also go, that we may die with Him'. So when Jesus came, He found that he had already been in the tomb four days. Now Bethany was near Jerusalem, about two miles away. And many of the Jews had joined the women around Martha and Mary, to comfort them concerning their brother. Now Martha, as soon as she heard that Jesus was coming, went and met Him, but Mary was sitting in the house. Now Martha said to Jesus, 'Lord, if You had been here, my brother would not have died. But even now I know that whatever You ask of God, God will give You.' Jesus said to her, 'Your brother will rise again'. Martha said to Him, 'I know that he will rise again

in the resurrection at the last day'. Jesus said to her, 'I am the resurrection and the life. He who believes in Me, though he may die, he shall live. And whoever lives and believes in Me shall never die. Do you believe this?' She said to Him, 'Yes, Lord, I believe that You are the Christ, the Son of God, who is to come into the world'. And when she had said these things, she went her way and secretly called Mary her sister, saying, 'The Teacher has come and is calling for you'. As soon as she heard that, she arose quickly and came to Him. Now Jesus had not yet come into the town, but was in the place where Martha met Him. Then the Jews who were with her in the house, and comforting her, when they saw that Mary rose up quickly and went out, followed her, saying, 'She is going to the tomb to weep there'. Then, when Mary came where Jesus was, and saw Him, she fell down at His feet, saying to Him, 'Lord, if You had been here, my brother would not have died'. Therefore, when Jesus saw her weeping, and the Jews who came with her weeping, He groaned in the spirit and was troubled. And He said, 'Where have you laid him?' They said to Him, 'Lord, come and see'. Jesus wept. Then the Jews said, 'See how He loved him!' And some of them said, 'Could not this Man, who opened the eyes of the blind, also have kept this man from dying?' Then Jesus, again groaning in Himself, came to the tomb. It was a cave, and a stone lay against it. Jesus said, 'Take away the stone'. Martha, the sister of him who was dead, said to Him, 'Lord, by this time there is a stench, for he has been dead four days'. Jesus said to her, 'Did I not say to you that if you would believe you would see the glory of God?' Then they took away the stone from the place where the dead man was lying. And Jesus lifted up His eyes and said, 'Father, I thank You that You have heard Me. And I know that You always hear Me, but because of the people who are standing by I said this, that they may believe that You sent Me'. Now when He had said these things, He cried with a loud voice, 'Lazarus, come forth!' And he who had died came out bound hand and foot with graveclothes, and his face was wrapped with a cloth. Jesus said to them, 'Loose him, and let him go'. Then many of the Jews who had come to Mary, and had seen the things Jesus did, believed in Him. But some of them went away to the Pharisees and told them the things Jesus did. Then the chief priests and the Pharisees gathered a council and said, 'What shall we do? For this Man works many signs. If we let Him alone like this, everyone will believe in Him, and the Romans will come and take away both our place and nation.' And one of them, Caiaphas, being high priest that year, said to them, 'You know nothing at all, nor do you consider that it is expedient for us that one man should die for the people, and not that the whole nation should perish'. Now this he did not say on his own authority; but being high priest that year he prophesied that Jesus would die for the nation, and not for that nation only, but also that He would gather together in one the children of God who were scattered abroad. Then, from that day on, they plotted to put Him to death.

John 11 verses 1-53

Once a Doctor has issued a death certificate, his relationship with the patient is at an end. Not so with this Physician. An example of this is seen in the Lord's relationship with Lazarus, His friend. Indeed, a Physician does not treat a friend - there is lack of objective assessment and treatment may misguided. But this is spiritual involvement with a perfect objective.

One would not have thought so however. The death of Lazarus was preventable. The Jews thought so,[159] Martha said so in verse 21 and Mary said so in verse 32. Yet the Lord allowed him to die; why? The glory of God through His Son - verse 4 - and to increase faith – verse 15. So Jesus waited two days where He was until Lazarus had died. He knew precisely when he had died – verse 11. Thomas thought the visit to Bethany was a suicide mission for everyone.[160]

In the resurrection of Lazarus, as noted, the Lord Jesus is not dealing with strangers but with a friend who had supported Him, given Him and His disciples hospitality and had come with his sisters to trust Him. This friendship was reciprocated as verse 5 of the chapter shows.

How many times has this chapter brought comfort to so many believers over the years! *"I am the resurrection and the life. He who believes in Me, though he may die, he shall live. And whoever lives and believes in Me shall never die"*, verses 25 and 26. In this statement, we have the fifth of the seven "I AMs" of John's Gospel. We have assurance of resurrection and immortality through the life of God within us when we believe and live in Jesus, 'The Life'.

Should we die physically, we will live again physically, and living physically presently with His life within, we shall never die spiritually because of that life of God within. Also in this statement, we surely see a cameo of 'the rapture' at the Lord's return.[161]

We witness here the deep empathy of Christ with Mary and Martha and the mourners, provoking the brief, deep, comment: *"Jesus wept"*. Could this be translated: 'He broke His heart'? Even the Jews observed the reality of His affection and said: *"Behold, how He loved him"*.

In contrast, observe the recorded weeping of the Lord on the Mount of Olives over the city of Jerusalem where the word for weeping is: 'lament'.[162] But this will be the place of His public return and vindication.[163] How different then when the King returns in power and glory! 'Then the shout will be Hosanna'.

But we also see His anger at the ravages of sin in death when: *"He groaned in the spirit and was troubled"*.[164] Suggestion has been made that the picture is of a warhorse going into battle. The Lord was doing battle with the forces of the Devil and death, Satan's powerful weapon.

By this time the body was in decay in a closed rock tomb. The disciples are instructed to remove the stone. The Lord prays in anticipation and Lazarus comes forth at His command: *"Lazarus, come forth!"* Remark has been made that had He not specified Lazarus by name, the graves would have all opened and all the dead raised! Lazarus comes out as he went in, bodily, via the opened entrance to the tomb. Corruption is reversed and he now has life. The Lord did not send His disciples into the tomb, the place of death, to assist Lazarus. He brought Lazarus out in life and power, *then* asked His disciples to help him. The disciples are to remove the grave clothes: *"Loose him, and let him go"* (verse 44). What the disciples could not do the Lord did. What they could do, He let them do. It is worthy of note that in His own resurrection, the Lord Jesus did not need anyone to remove *His* grave clothes. He folded His napkin and left His grave clothes, which He had transcended, behind in the tomb. He needed no open grave to get out, but to let others see and enter in. His resurrection was to a new order. *"I am He who lives, and was dead, and behold, I am alive for evermore. Amen."*[165]

What care to remove the grave clothes would be required! Lazarus had life but he needed help. How were the grave clothes removed? Slowly and with care. They would be sticking to him. Similarly, with a new person in Christ, such have to be dealt with carefully. New life is present but it takes care and patience for the "old grave clothes" to be removed and for the new robe of righteousness, freely given by God the Father, to be displayed. Lazarus does not speak. One would be anxious to hear of his experience after death. How we love the spectacular and unusual! Many questions could have been asked about 'the other side'. But that is hidden from us. Interestingly, Paul is not permitted to tell of the Third Heaven in 2 Corinthians 12. The Lord has told us He is away to prepare a place for us and that He will return and receive us to Himself.[166] We are to trust and live by the revealed light of God and have faith in His promise, power and purpose.

We next read of the resurrected Lazarus in the following chapter of John's Gospel. He is reclining beside his friend, now Saviour, at supper table. Martha, his sister, is in uncomplaining attendance; Mary is about to pour oil of spikenard over the feet of the Lord Jesus in worship. Many people come to this house to see Lazarus as well as Jesus, verse 9. Again, no word is recorded from Lazarus, but his visible presence is enough testimony to the power of resurrection of the Lord Jesus. Sometimes words are superfluous; his new life is the story.

This powerful miracle sealed the death of Jesus, as we read in verses 47 and 48. The chief priests and Pharisees held a council because of His popularity and power, the High Priest making a prophecy of dramatic irony that *"One man should die for the people"*.[167] Did he use Urim and Thumim for this?[168] It was true in a sense he did not realise.

The life of Lazarus was also threatened.[169] The Jews sought to put Lazarus to death - a man that had newly been raised from the dead! How blind and prejudiced is unbelief! This was because of him so many of the Jews now believed in Jesus. Indeed, we read in Chapter 12 verse 17 that people who saw the miracle accompanied Jesus and His disciples into Jerusalem in triumphal procession bearing witness (with others who had come up from Galilee). People who had heard of the miracle in Jerusalem also came out of the city to meet Him with palm branches and celebrated His entry into the city as the Son of David. Events had now reached a climax.

What a cost to the Lord emotionally, spiritually and physically was this mighty work! It is the seventh sign recorded by John in his Gospel. The seven signs recorded before the Cross to present Jesus as the Son of God are now completed. The first was at a wedding where the Lord brought joy, the last at a cemetery where He reverses sorrow for joy. The eighth will be after His resurrection in John 21. Lazarus would die again but the person who dies in Jesus today will be raised in power with an incorruptible body like His body of glory.[170] What a blessed prospect! Death has lost its sting in the glorious resurrection of the *"Firstborn from among the dead"*[171] and the *"Firstfruits of all who sleep"*.[172]

In the three recorded resurrections, there is a progression of thought. The young girl aged twelve was in her sick bed, in her own house, newly dead. The young man, in his open coffin on the way to his grave, was obviously some hours dead. Lazarus in his grave and in corruption was four days dead. All are raised to life but will die again. When we are raised to life, we shall never die. Amazing!

Alfred Edersheim gives interesting insight to the Jewish thought regarding the time and manner of death at the time of our Lord.[173] Sudden death was called:

- "being swallowed up";
- death after one day's illness was that of "rejection"; after two days, that of "despair";
- after four days, that of "reproof";
- after five days "a natural death".

No matter the divisions of time, the One who said: *"I am the resurrection and the life"* is able for every circumstance beyond the veil of death.

How great the saying of Jesus: *"The hour is coming, and now is, when the dead shall hear the voice of the Son of God; and those who hear will live. For as the Father has life in Himself, so He has granted to the Son to have life in Himself ... The hour is coming in which all who are in the graves will hear His voice and come forth – those who have done good, to the resurrection of life, and those who have done evil, to the resurrection of condemnation"*.[174]

The Lord Jesus demonstrates in His earthly life His power to prevent death. No one can die in the presence of the Prince of Life. He even had to be the first of the three to die on the Cross. But His power to raise the dead, no matter the circumstances and duration of death, is something beyond the ability of any Physician.

It is worthy of note that the Lord resurrected the complete person; spirit, soul and body. Resurrection will be experienced by all believers if the Lord does not return first, in which case some believers will not experience death before glory. But to what end? The dead in Christ will awake to everlasting life and resurrection power with redeemed bodies to reign with Christ, the Prince of life. But what of the unrighteous dead? They will be raised also, but to everlasting shame and contempt.[175] Jesus said that if we do not believe *"That I Am"*, we will die in our sins, and where He is we cannot come.[176] Solemn thought!

Death is not the end but the beginning of an end without end.

---

[146]Leviticus 13

[147]Stedman A.M.M, *"Greek Testament Selections"*, Methuen and Co., London, 1905 page 131: "Free my arms that I may heal the wounded servant."

[148]Mark 5 verse 41

[149]John 18 verse 10, Luke 8 verse 53, John 11 verse 11, Luke 8 verse 55

[150]St. John, Harold, *"An Analysis of the Gospel of Mark"*, Gospel Folio Press, page 75

[151]Isaiah 42 verse 3

[152]Genesis 49 verse 15

[153]1 Samuel 28

[154]Edersheim A., Vol.1, page 556

[155]Edersheim A.: "In Galilee the hired mourners followed the bier. First came the women. As woman brought death into the world, women ought to lead the way in the funeral procession." *"Sketches of Jewish Social Life"*, page 156, Hendrickson Publishers

[156]Ruth 4 verse 5

[157]Crawford N: *"The intransitive use of the verb is rare save in medical writings"* in "Luke", *"What the Bible Teaches"* page 121, quoting A. Plummer.

[158]Crawford N. " Luke", *"What the Bible Teaches"*, page 122, quoting W. Liefeld.

[159]John 11 verse 37

[160]John 11 verse 16

[161]1 Thessalonians 4 verses 13-18

[162]Luke 19 verse 41

[163]Zechariah 14 verse 4; Acts 1 verse 11

[164]John 11 verse 33

[165]Revelation 1 verse 18
[166]John 14 verses 1 & 2
[167]John 18 verse 14
[168]Exodus 28 verse 30
[169]John 12 verses 10 & 11
[170]1 Corinthians 15; Philippians 3 verse 21
[171]Colossians 1 verses 18
[172]1 Corinthians 15 verse 20
[173]Edersheim, Alfred, *"Sketches of Jewish Social Life"*, [updated edition] page 153, Hendrickson Publishers
[174]John 5 verses 35, 26, 28 and 29.
[175]Daniel 12 verse 2
[176]John 8 verses 21 and 24

From Private Cases to Public and Social Medicine

It is noteworthy that the Lord Jesus did not deal with Public Health issues. He could have suggested a National Health plan to reduce disease in the country, a better diet for all or new sanitation laws for urban communities, better housing facilities for the poor to reduce infant mortality rates, commented on bogus medical practices or lack of hospital care at Bethesda in Jerusalem.

No doubt child labour would occur and there would be homelessness - He Himself had often to sleep outdoors. He could have praised Pilate for his new aqueduct construction programme to bring needed fresh water into Jerusalem but He did not. Nor did He condemn him for his method of raising the finance for the project, *i.e.* robbing the Temple treasury!

He could have approached the religious authorities for a stricter enforcement of the Law of Moses against divorce and promiscuity among the clergy[177] and the immoral state of the nation[178] but did not. He was working under the Law and personally fulfilling the Law, upholding the Law, preaching the spirit of the Law, not lobbying to have Mosaic Law enforcement.

He did not seek to introduce stricter safety laws after the collapse of the tower of Siloam or subsequently suggest an 'Accident Prevention Week'.

He did not insist His disciples wash before eating, as what was practised by other disciples of Rabbis was traditional ritual washing, not a matter of hygiene. He was more concerned with what came out of a person morally. Yet, it is pointed out by Jewish guides in Israel today that Jesus was never reported as ever entering the city of Tiberius. Created by Herod Antipas, it was made the capital of Galilee instead of the Roman city Sepphoris. But the town was built on a graveyard. No Jewish Rabbi would, therefore, enter it. It was defiled.

On the two occasions when He fed a multitude of people, the disciples gathered up all the left-over scraps. This would have taken longer than it took to feed them. But you would never have known thousands of people were there having a picnic in the countryside. He was environmentally conscious., no litter remained.

He supplied miraculously enough top quality wine for a wedding banquet but never preached on the social consequences of alcohol, an ever pertinent problem. But He did not condone indulgence either although He was accused of such, and of eating too much, a scurrilous remark made by His enemies. By repeatedly exorcising demons, He was improving the spiritual and mental state of society but did not have a mental health campaign.

He did not speak of the effect of the Roman occupation on health and wealth or the abuse by some soldiers of their power as John the Baptist did. In fact, if Matthew 5 verses 39-42 is a veiled reference to the unlawful action of soldiers in the community, the emphasis is on the right *reaction* to them by His followers. The life-style of Herod is not mentioned save when the Lord was told he was out to kill Him. He then revealed His private view of him as *"That fox"*.[179] He did not condemn the Zealot movement or support it. He chose a Zealot as one of the disciples, Simon by name, but for spiritual training in the Kingdom of God. He crosses national and religious and social taboos in His relationship with the Samaritans. He did not condemn slavery as practised in Israel at that time. He refused to mediate on family inheritance rights or workers' rights regarding wages.[180] He did not interfere with the taxation laws regarding the Roman occupation.[181] He spoke of corrupt accountants and judges with self-interest but He Himself made no judgment on them. In fact, He says His disciples could learn spiritual lessons from the accountant's shrewdness![182]

He strongly upheld God's original concept of marriage by attending the wedding at Cana of Galilee in John 2 and by His teaching on marriage in Matthew 5 verse 31 and Matthew 19 verses 3-12. He emphasised the responsibility of families to care for their elderly parents[183] and the importance of the proper attitude to and care of children.[184] He gave to the poor from the common purse,[185] advised the resolution of disputes privately, on the great benefits of forgiveness and the pointlessness of worry. All of these have personal, social and health implications.

He diagnosed the state of the Nation in Matthew 13 verses 13-15 better than any politician or national religious leader - the people's heart was calloused. It was a wicked and adulterous generation. They refused to repent and change. The city of Jerusalem by its rejection of Him was facing ruin. Also the Temple with its architectural glory would be razed to the ground. A humanitarian crisis would soon be upon the nation.

The Lord had the right and power to bring in a just and moral society in His lifetime but He did not. Why? As He stated, His Kingdom was not of this world. He had come to preach the Kingdom of God which was and still is in the midst of society. In the synagogue at Nazareth at the beginning of His ministry, Jesus publicly announces His purpose for people.[186] It is clearly a personal message of repentance toward God and faith in Him. Men and women need to be changed first from within. Health would come as a consequence both socially and personally. Hence His mission to preach the Gospel, make disciples and send them also to preach this life-changing message.

If people are not changed in their heart, legislation for social change will be superficial in effect. Also enforced religion will be skin-deep and lack life and power. The vertical relationship with God comes before the lateral relationship with people.

---

[177]John 8 verse 3
[178]Matthew 16 verse 4
[179]Luke 13 verse 32
[180]Matthew 20 verses 1-16
[181]Luke 20 verse 25
[182]See Luke 16
[183]Matthew 15 verses 3-9
[184]Matthew 18 verses 1-5, 10 and Chapter 19 verse 14
[185]John 12 verses 5,6; John 13 verse 29
[186]Luke 4 verses 18-19

Epilogue

I have sought to categorise some of the healing miracles of the Lord Jesus from a modern perspective.

One cannot examine or exhaust all the Medical Miracles of our Lord. John says toward the close of his Gospel *"Truly Jesus did many other signs in the presence of His disciples, which are not written in this book; but these are written that you may believe that Jesus is the Christ, the Son of God, and that believing you may have life in His name."*

To God be the Glory